# Fire of God

While every precaution has been taken in the preparation of this book, the publisher assumes no responsibility for errors or omissions, or for damages resulting from the use of the information contained herein.

FIRE OF GOD

**First edition. December 1, 2021.**

Copyright © 2021 Riaan Engelbrecht.

ISBN: 979-8215656495

Written by Riaan Engelbrecht.

# Table of Contents

To God be the glory. And to my wife, Lynette, thank you for all your motivation, inspiration and strength.

Spirit-filled souls are ablaze for God. They love with a love that glows. They serve with a faith that kindles. They serve with a devotion that consumes. They hate sin with a fierceness that burns. They rejoice with a joy that radiates. Love is perfected in the fire of God.

**Samuel Chadwick**

# Let it burn

The words of David Ruis during the Toronto Revival still ring true in my heart today: "Let it burn! Yes, Lord, let it burn!"

Years ago, I remember someone asking me what all this talk about the fire of God is. I was still young in the faith. Hardly out of my spiritual nappies. But I was on fire for God! I had met my Saviour, and He had led me from darkness to the light! I was enjoying as a South African citizen, the afterglow of revivals such as the one in Toronto. Vineyard Worship was big in those days. Catch the fire was the talk of the town among the Charismatics and even Pentecostals. Believers were talking about the 'fire' of God. Some in the church had no clue what this "fire" was all about. Some regarded it with great scepticism, calling it another phase, or another spiritual fashion or a fad.

When asked the question, I was slightly shocked. After all, who doesn't know the fire of God? Or at least, so I thought at the time. Back then, somewhat two decades ago, I was still very naïve when it came to the church and the state of believers. I thought everyone was filled with the Spirit. I thought everyone was on fire for God. I thought everyone was walking in the manifested glory of God and was doing great work for the Kingdom. Of course, this was far from reality. Reality is, and still today, there are still many believers who have not even been filled by the Spirit or who have not even reached a point of being on fire for God.

So what is this fire? It is the very presence of God. It is that simple. It is the presence through the indwelling of the Holy Spirit. It is the anointing of the Spirit of God. It is the flow of the power of the Spirit of God. The fire, however, is not something detached from God. It is not something that you can manipulate, being one of the five elements (for then we are dabbling in paganism and witchcraft).

On the Day of Pentecost, we read that tongues of fire rested upon the disciples. Such fire was the manifested presence of the Holy Spirit that was promised by Jesus. It is the Spirit of power, of which we read in Acts 1:8. Isaiah 11:2 speaks of the Spirit of wisdom, understanding, knowledge, counsel and might. To speak of the fire speaks of the indwelling burning of the presence of the Holy Spirit. It speaks of the holy and divine presence of the Spirit of God, thus the Ruach Elohim, who comes to empower, equip and saturate the disciples with the Word and Truth of God (John 16). Exodus 24:17 says, "To the Israelites the glory of the LORD looked like a consuming fire on top of the mountain." Oh yes, our God is a consuming fire (Hebrews 12:29)!

One cannot understand the fire without knowing the Holy Spirit. The Spirit is the fire. The Spirit is the truth of Jesus. How do you truly know the fire of God without knowing the Spirit of God? How can one know of the fire that burns deep within without knowing the Spirit who brings life? So when someone asks what this fire is, it cannot be explained in theological terms. It is your spirit connecting with the Holy Spirit and being set on fire. It is your soul being saturated with the majesty and greatness of God and thus set on fire by an all-consuming God. It is a fire that burns in your bones, in your heart and spirit. For anybody who has been reborn (John 3) must surely walk by the Spirit of God, and thus by the fire of God.

For just as a fire rages and can so easily consume wood and paper, just so the more we yield and submit to God the more the fire will burn. For fire needs fuel. We are the fuel as living sacrifices seeking God (Romans 12:1). For as a fire is wild and intense, so we become wild and intense for God. For as fire is powerful and dangerous, so in Christ we become powerful and dangerous for the Kingdom fighting the darkness. For as a fire does not easily surrender, so we must not easily surrender to the enemy but keep fighting the good fight

(Ephesians 6). Yes, it is the fire of God. It is the fire that brings us closer in union with God. It must be a fire that consumes us so that we cannot but tell the world of God, His goodness, love and mercy!

When we speak of the fire of God, we can also speak of the light of God, for fire is light. All light has a source. Something must create light. In the case of the Lord's light, He is the source as an all-consuming fire. In Aramaic, "fire" can be translated as "consuming light." Even in the natural realm, light always has a source. The light of the day comes from the fire of the sun. Light is a product of a power source—a fire. Anyone in Biblical times who heard the word "light" would automatically know that it was also a reference to fire because fire was always the source of light.

Light is the product of fire. The only difference is that light can be seen from a long distance compared to when the fire can be felt. Light is a signal, but fire is the source. For Christians to be "in" the Lord, they must be in His fire to produce the light and the heat of His love and glory. The Bible teaches that we must be Holy as He is Holy (1 Peter 1:16). How does the Bible teach to be Holy? We must be refined by His fire (1 Peter 1:7). His fire is spiritual, not natural. Therefore, we must be consumed by His fire to be made holy so that we may shine His light in this dark world!

We may ask how can we say "holy fire" if the exact words are not found in the Bible? It's very simple. Is the Lord holy? Yes. Is the Lord an all-consuming fire? Yes. Must we say holy all-consuming fire? No, it's understood that He is both holy and all-consuming. He is also many other things, such as Righteousness, Love, Truth, and The Way. We need not refer to all of His attributes when we speak of Him. So let the holy fire consume us as we seek to be holy as He is holy!

The Lord said, "I came to bring fire" (Luke 12:49). He is not talking about a natural fire. The Word of God must always be understood in a spiritual context. Therefore, the Lord is speaking about His fire—His holy and spiritual fire. In the same chapter, the Lord said, "51 Do you suppose that I came to give peace on earth? I tell you, not at all, but rather division. 52 For from now on five in one house will be divided: three against two, and two against three. 53 Father will be divided against son and son against father, mother against daughter and daughter against mother, mother-in-law against her daughter-in-law and daughter-in-law against her mother-in-law."

In light of Luke 12, the fire of God brings separation. A separation from the light and dark, from the good and the wicked, from the moral and the immoral, from the holy and the unholy, from the common and the uncommon and the pure from the impure. It brings separation between the just and the unjust and the Spirit and the flesh.

For such is the nature of the fire, for it is the blazing presence of the Spirit who leads us in all truth (John 16). And such truth is the Word of which we read of in Hebrews 4, "12 For the word of God is living and powerful, and sharper than any two-edged sword, piercing even to the division of soul and spirit, and of joints and marrow, and is a discerner of the thoughts and intents of the heart. 13 And there is no creature hidden from His sight, but all things are naked and open to the eyes of Him to whom we must give account."

Just as all is naked in vulnerability to the flames of a fire, just so we cannot hide from the truth of the Word. Adam and Eve were left naked in the presence of God's truth when they sinned, and just so we cannot from the truth of God. Jesus spoke of a fire that came by the indwelling of the baptism of the Spirit. Bu such a fire within the believer, we are set on fire for God and we now burn with God's truth, righteousness, justice and morality! By such truth, we are sanctified (John 17:17), thus set apart and divided from darkness, carnality and lies. Jesus warned of the great separation even in households not just in the world simply because some will be willing to embrace the Spirit, thus the truth of the Word and the sanctifying power of the fire of His presence, while others will resist or deny or ignore or rebel against it.

2 Corinthians 6:14 (KJV) says, "Be ye not unequally yoked together with unbelievers, for what fellowship hath righteousness with unrighteousness? And what communion hath light with darkness?"

The fire is the light and the light shines in the darkness for those who believe. We read in "1 John 1: 5 This is the message which we have heard from Him and declare to you, that God is light and in Him is no darkness at all. 6 If we say that we have fellowship with Him, and walk in darkness, we lie and do not practice the truth. 7 But if we walk in the light as He is in the light, we have fellowship with one another, and the blood of Jesus Christ His Son cleanses us from all sin." There will be division in this world because many will reject the light, therefore Jesus who is the light of the world, while others will seek the fire and the light of God's truth, purity and holiness. There is simply no fellowship between those who choose the light and those who choose the darkness, for one chooses the truth and the other deception. And such fire was poured out on Pentecost, and so we have to decide what we choose.

If a Christian never felt the Lord's fire before, then how would he know whether he is experiencing it or not? Humility is the key. Believers must examine if they are truly born again of the Holy Spirit (2 Corinthians 13:5). Once born again of the Holy Spirit, they will begin to understand the Word of God in a spiritual sense and no longer need to rely on a natural sense. This is what the Lord meant when He said to the disciples in John 16:13, that when the Spirit of Truth, the Holy Spirit, would come to them, He would guide them into all truth.

That means that truth cannot be understood without the impartation of the Holy Spirit because He is the Spirit of Truth. When the Spirit of Truth guides a Christian through the Word of God, then they will no longer experience the frustration of trying to interpret the Word of God in a literal sense. We must be willing to yield and submit to God, only seeing His light, and to remain in Him.

# Intimate Fires of the Lord

*Psalm 63: 1 O God, You are my God; early will I seek You; My soul thirsts for You; My flesh longs for You in a dry and thirsty land where there is no water. 2 So I have looked for You in the sanctuary, to see Your power and Your glory. 3 Because Your lovingkindness is better than life, My lips shall praise You. 4 Thus I will bless You while I live; I will lift up my hands in Your name. 5 My soul shall be satisfied as with marrow and fatness, and my mouth shall praise You with joyful lips*

As we draw closer to the Father in union of spirit, so we draw closer to the fire of His presence that burns in the Holy of Holies. And in the burning, we are dangerous in our love, in our faith and our hope. In union, the fire of the Lord shines through and in us, marking our path and casting light in the darkness. Just as a man that holds a lit candle when standing in the velvet blackness, just so does the Word and Presence of the Lord serve as an emanating light to illuminate our spirit and soul.

When such a flame dies, then we stand in the darkness and do not know where to tread. When we walk in darkness, we can't lead anybody else out of the darkness. For we are the blind leading the blind. Let us not be fooled or be deceived: such light will only shine when we constantly and with reverent fear draw closer to Him and seek to obey Him. Let us not be fooled into thinking that if we choose to do the things of the Lord and do the things of this world, the candle will remain lit.

No, for the fire will die and then we will be stranded in darkness, ignorant and disoriented. For the Lord asks this question: what extinguishes any fire? Lack of oxygen and heat kills the flame. The Lord is the oxygen and heat. If we fail to obey and submit, then we walk not in His light. For it is written that if we love the Lord, then we will obey Him. Unrighteousness kills oxygen and heat. Ezekiel 18 (v 24-29) makes it clear that we must not be so arrogant as to think we can walk in His light and also try to please this world. This is confirmed by Hebrews 6 (v4-7). We will fall in greater iniquity because of such arrogance and ignorance.

There is a true danger for those who walk in unrighteousness, even though seeking union with God. This simply cannot be. This makes a mockery and a disgrace of the Lord's death on the cross since we abuse grace that has led us out of Egypt. We must make a dangerous stand for the truth: either live for the Lord, completely and utterly or choose the world. The Lord's flame will only burn bright in us if we walk in righteousness. Such a path we can only follow if we seek true union with the Lord, but this requires obedience, submission and abandonment unto the cross and a willingness to die unto the self.

The Lord is calling His children to walk in true righteousness, in purity and love so that the flame can burn and the darkness be driven back. Too many flames have died or are dying because of the lack of oxygen or heat. Let us not be so arrogant. Let us be not so wise. Let us return to Him in reverent fear. We must be so hungry for His fire that we must seek to be baptised in the pure fire of holiness, so let us become like burning torches for the nations. Indeed, the fire of suffering brings forth the gold of purity and none of us as believers will be purified except by the fire of inward pain.

Yet, where the baptism of the Holy Spirit produces the truth, so the fire produces suffering. This allows us to grow purer and holier. Such holiness and purity lead to a greater spiritual plateau, drawing us closer to God, opening the way for us to dwell in the blessed state of spiritual unity and divine love. Such is the path of the dangerous disciple.

We need to willingly surrender and seek the Lord's fire. We, therefore, have to open our spirit, soul, and body so that God can examine the deepest recesses of our existence, entering into the deepest chamber of our spirit and soul. We will find a divine working of God's Wisdom, Love and Power to cleanse and renew us. We have to move in faith, believing God is working to transform us more into the likeness of His Son.

In the Bible, the fire of God is seen as one of judgment. The divine fire is therefore the fire that purifies us through His judgment so that we can see God. The key to such examination by God and for the fire to purify is complete abandonment in soul and spirit and body before God (complete surrender). When we abandon ourselves, we lay before the cross our rights, ambitions, desires, fears, weaknesses, sin, calling, purposes (our entire life) so that God will fill us. In abandonment, we allow God to captivate us, allowing God to be our true King, and our desires and ambitions come in complete submission to God's purposes for us. Abandonment is our white flag of surrender, not wishing to resist God on any level or in any way. With resistance comes rebellion, so we stop fighting God, but now work with Him. From abandonment flows a dangerous love and faith in the impossible.

The continual process of abandonment allows for God's divine fire to consume us, for we are now vessels that are submitted in the hands of the Lord. This fire produces inward suffering, since God's fire reveals to us through Wisdom, Power and Love, our much deeper impurities, longings and failures. It is these impurities and the guilt and shame of our failures that prevent us from engaging in a far more mature and intimate relationship with God. There is therefore painful inward suffering that we have to endure when baptised by fire, for we are confronted with the deeper evils of our soul, realizing that the dragons of the darkness in our inner being have to be slain.

Seeking the divine fire is, therefore, our complete abandonment before God, as we willingly seek to lay down our sinful nature for the sake of gaining God's love. Without the revelation of the fire, we will tend to examine ourselves inwardly. The problem is that we so often deceive ourselves, while we do the true effect of God's refining will never be experienced. The fire of God both purifies and judges. When God's fire dwells in our inner chambers of the spirit and the soul, we are exposed to God's judgment. The dragons (sin, evil, failures) of our life are exposed by the pure fire so that we can address them, to be purified and cleansed.

The indwelling fire involves not only the complete abandonment of the self, but it also involves the complete mortification of the deeds of the sinful nature (Romans 8). To mortify means to put to death. To mortify the deeds of the sinful nature means to depart, get rid of, and overcome the sinful nature. God's fire grants us the grace, love, and power to set us free. We, however, have to face our dragons, and with God's love and wisdom, mortify them. There is also a suffering produced by the process of mortification, for it is painful and direct when we mortify the deeds of the sinful nature.

Mortification is the process of going to the cross and nailing to the rugged tree our sins and all that opposes God. The cross is painful, but it is the victory over death. The cross is life and freedom in Jesus. The cleansing and purifying fire purifies and mortifies, as we are forced to confront the dragons that dwell deep within us. Through purification and mortification (made possible by abandonment), we become holier and purer. To be holy and pure produces righteousness that produces godliness, as we are constantly refined to become like gold in character and nature (noble use to the Lord Almighty).

In such a state of greater godliness and purity, we are drawn closer to the Lord Almighty. We allow for the complete melting of our spirit and soul into the divine presence of the Lord, fully carrying the cross and denying ourselves. Abandonment, mortification and purification draw us into the deepest chambers of God's throne room. This is where the divine spiritual presence of the Lord is found in the Holy of Holies. It is within the Holy of Holies where God dwells in His full glory, splendour, and majesty.

The Kingdom of God is also within us through the Spirit of the Living God; therefore the Holy of Holies is within the deepest chambers of our spirit and soul. For us to dwell with God in this place of peace and love, we need to be cleansed and purified so that we can dwell within the Holy of Holies. In the Holy of Holies, we allow God to be the very ultimate centre of our lives, refined by His divine Love, led by His Wisdom and driven by His awesome power. Seeking the fire and letting it dwell is not only a one-day process. It is a continuous process of abandonment, mortification, and purification. The suffering that is produced is therefore also continuous and painful, as we are constantly being deeply examined and refined by the fire of the Almighty God.

To seek the fire is to seek the deeper realms of God, but it also means surrendering to the suffering and living completely for God. It is painful to completely surrender our desires, ambitions, and pleasures, letting God become divinely united with our spirit and soul. Such suffering, however, must be done with perseverance and humility, as we continue to draw closer to God, in reverence, abiding in the love of God and the resurrection power of the Blood of Christ. In essence, God has to be glorified, and the flesh and soul mortified.

But we always have choices. We can choose our level of abandonment, our level of mortification, and how much we seek to be purified. To reach the inner chambers of God's throne room, we must never hesitate in our mortification, but let God's power and fire refine and set us free from our inner turmoil and dragons.

It is only when we discover the inner path, which leads to God's wonderful presence, that the power of the external world in terms of interest and its power of bondage is broken. We must turn to God who is within us so that God can, through divine unity, bring forth healing and deliverance.

Out of such a state of brokenness and intimacy flows a deep, dangerous desire to see a broken world healed, delivered and set free by the radical and dangerous love of God. For God is radical, beautiful and full of mercy and grace.

May we arise in God's splendour to His Glory. May His radical love consume us, change and renew us so that this caged world may know the liberating power of His mercy and grace.

# From the altars of the patriarchs to the flames of Pentecost

One of the most powerful themes that runs through all of Scripture is the fire of God. From Genesis to Revelation, God's fire appears again and again. It burns in bushes, descends upon altars, rests upon mountains, fills temples, empowers prophets, and ultimately comes to dwell within believers through the Holy Spirit.

Yet many believers misunderstand the fire of God. Some see it merely as emotional excitement. Others associate it only with revival meetings or manifestations of power. But in Scripture, the fire of God is far deeper. God's fire represents His holy presence, His glory, His purity, His power, His judgment, His zeal, His love, and His transforming work. The story of redemption can almost be traced through the movement of divine fire.

The first appearances of God's fire are closely connected to sacrifice and worship. Throughout Genesis, the patriarchs built altars. Noah built an altar after the Flood. Abraham built altars wherever God appeared. Isaac built altars. Jacob built altars. An altar represented a meeting place between God and man. Though Scripture does not always explicitly mention fire falling on these early altars, the principle is established: where there is sacrifice, there is divine encounter. This principle continues throughout Scripture. God's fire is drawn to surrender. The altar becomes the place where heaven touches earth.

1

This is why the New Testament calls believers living sacrifices because the fire always seeks an altar.

The next great revelation comes in Exodus 3. Moses encounters God in a bush that burns yet is not consumed. This is one of the most profound pictures of God's nature. The bush burns continuously. Yet it remains intact. God reveals Himself through supernatural fire. The lesson is extraordinary. God's fire does not merely destroy, it transforms. Natural fire consumes and leaves ashes, yet divine fire consumes and leaves glory. The bush becomes a picture of redeemed humanity. Apart from God, man is consumed by sin. But when God inhabits a vessel, His presence burns within it without destroying it. The bush carried the fire because God was in it. Likewise, believers become vessels carrying divine fire because God Himself dwells within them.

At Mount Sinai, the fire of God appears on a national scale. The mountain trembles. Thunder roars. Lightning flashes. Smoke ascends. Fire descends from heaven. The mountain becomes an earthly throne room. Exodus tells us that Mount Sinai was altogether in smoke, because the LORD descended upon it in fire.

This fire revealed several aspects of God's nature. The people could not casually approach the mountain. Boundaries were established because sinful man could not simply rush into God's presence. The fire proclaimed: God is holy. The mountain shook because creation itself responded to its Creator. Fire became a visible manifestation of divine kingship. God was not merely displaying power; He was establishing a relationship. The fire accompanied the giving of the covenant. God was entering into a covenantal union with His people.

After Sinai, God's fire moved with Israel. By night, He appeared as a pillar of fire. This fire had several functions. The fire showed Israel where to go. The fire also stood between Israel and their enemies as protection. The fire signified that God was among His people. The lesson remains powerful. The fire of God was never intended merely to be experienced. It was intended to be followed. Many seek manifestations, yet God seeks obedience. The fire moved, and Israel had to move with it.

One of the most important moments occurs when the Tabernacle is dedicated. Fire falls from heaven and consumes the sacrifice. The heavenly fire ignites the altar. Then God gives a remarkable command: "The fire shall ever be burning upon the altar; it shall never go out." This becomes a prophetic picture. The fire originated from God, because man did not create it. Man's responsibility was to maintain it. Likewise, spiritual fire originates in God. Revival cannot be manufactured, anointing cannot be manufactured, and the Holy Spirit cannot be manufactured. Heaven provides the fire and so believers are called to steward it.

On Mount Carmel, Elijah confronts the prophets of Baal. The false prophets cry out for hours. Nothing happens. Then Elijah repairs the broken altar. Notice the order: first the altar, then the sacrifice, and then the fire. Fire fell only after the altar was restored. This remains true spiritually. Many seek fire while neglecting the altar. God often seeks to rebuild the altar of surrender before releasing fresh fire. The fire consumed the sacrifice, the wood, the stones, and the water. Nothing could resist God's fire. This revealed God's supremacy.

When Solomon dedicated the Temple, fire again descended from heaven. The glory of God filled the house and the priests could not stand to minister. Here we see another principle: fire and glory are connected. Fire is often the visible manifestation and glory is the divine reality behind it. Where God's fire burns, His glory is revealed.

As the Old Testament progresses, the symbolism becomes increasingly internal. Jeremiah 20:9 says, "His word was in mine heart as a burning fire shut up in my bones." The fire is no longer merely external. It burns within. This anticipates the New Covenant. God's presence will move from buildings into people. The fire will no longer remain on mountains and altars, but it will dwell inside human hearts.

John the Baptist announces a coming baptism. He declares in Matthew 3:11, "He shall baptize you with the Holy Ghost and with fire." This statement becomes a bridge between the Old and New Covenants. Everything the Old Testament fire symbolised now begins to converge in Christ. The Messiah would not merely reveal God's fire. He would impart it.

Acts 2 is perhaps the most dramatic fulfilment of the fire motif. The disciples gather in the upper room. Suddenly, a mighty rushing wind appears, tongues of fire descend, and the Spirit fills each believer. This event mirrors Sinai in astonishing ways. At Sinai, fire descended on a mountain and God gave His Law. At Pentecost, fire descended on people, and God wrote His Law upon hearts. At Sinai, fire rested upon a place. At Pentecost, fire rested upon persons. The mountain became a man and the temple became a people. The dwelling place of God shifted from stone structures to living vessels. This is one of the greatest transitions in Scripture; God's fire no longer merely visits, but His fire inhabits.

The writer of Hebrews in chapter 12:29 quotes Deuteronomy: "Our God is a consuming fire." This is one of the most important descriptions of God in all Scripture. Notice it does not merely say God has fire. It says that God is fire. Not literal physical fire, but fire as a description of His nature. What does this mean?

Everything contrary to God's nature is burned away. Impurity cannot survive His presence. Pride cannot survive His presence. Rebellion cannot survive His presence. The closer we draw to Him, the more these things are exposed.

Gold is purified in fire, yet the fire does not destroy the gold. It removes impurities. Likewise, God's fire refines believers. Trials often become furnaces through which God purifies faith. The goal is not destruction, but transformation.

The fire of God is not merely judgment. It is passion. The love of God burns with holy intensity. The Song of Songs speaks of love as "A most vehement flame." In Song of Solomon 8:6, the phrase "a most vehement flame" (translated in some versions as "a blazing fire" or "a most intense flame") means that true love is an all-consuming, unstoppable, and divinely sparked force. It represents the emotional and spiritual climax of the entire book, defining love as an unquenchable power that cannot be bought, forced, or destroyed. God's fire ignites hearts with love for Him. The disciples were transformed after Pentecost. Fearful men became fearless witnesses. Weak men became mighty ambassadors. The fire empowered them for the mission.

Under the New Covenant, the symbolism reaches its climax. The believer becomes the temple, the altar, the sacrifice, and the vessel. Paul writes, "Present your bodies a living sacrifice." The altar is no longer constructed of stones. It is the surrendered life. The fire that once burned upon the altar now burns within the believer.

The greatest gift to believers is not power. It is God's presence Himself. The fire signifies that God dwells among His people. The Spirit continually works to conform believers into Christ's image because the fire removes what does not belong. The fire also awakens hunger for God. Cold religion cannot survive where divine fire burns. Fire gives light, and just so, the Holy Spirit enlightens understanding and reveals truth. Pentecostal fire produces a courageous witness. The purpose of fire is not excitement, but Christlikeness.

The Bible begins with a flaming sword guarding Eden. It continues with burning bushes, fiery mountains, blazing altars, fiery pillars, and tongues of fire. It ends with God dwelling among His people forever. The fire that once appeared externally ultimately becomes internal. The fire that rested upon altars comes to rest upon hearts. The fire that descended on Sinai descends at Pentecost. The God who revealed Himself through fire now dwells within His people through the Holy Spirit. The great question for every believer is not merely: "Have I experienced the fire?" But rather: "Am I becoming a vessel that can continually carry it?" For God's ultimate purpose has never been merely to visit His people with fire, but to make them living temples in whom His holy fire burns continually, illuminating the world, purifying the heart, revealing His glory, and preparing a Bride fit for the presence of the One who is forever called: "Our God, a consuming fire."

# Keeping the fires burning

To truly understand how to keep the fires burning within our spirit and soul (God's presence), we visit "Leviticus 6: The Law of the Burnt Offering: 8 Then the LORD spoke to Moses, saying, 9 "Command Aaron and his sons, saying, 'This is the law of the burnt offering: The burnt offering shall be on the hearth upon the altar all night until morning, and the fire of the altar shall be kept burning on it. 10 And the priest shall put on his linen garment, and his linen trousers he shall put on his body, and take up the ashes of the burnt offering which the fire has consumed on the altar, and he shall put them beside the altar. 11 Then he shall take off his garments, put on other garments, and carry the ashes outside the camp to a clean place. 12 And the fire on the altar shall be kept burning on it; it shall not be put out. And the priest shall burn wood on it every morning, and lay the burnt offering in order on it; and he shall burn on it the fat of the peace offerings. 13 A fire shall always be burning on the altar; it shall never go out."

In Leviticus 6, the Lord commanded the priests to keep the fires on the altar burning – this was a sign of the continuous presence of the Lord (Numbers 15). The burnt offering is one of the oldest and most common offerings in history. It's entirely possible that Abel's offering in Genesis 4:4 was a burnt offering, although the first recorded instance is in Genesis 8:20 when Noah offers burnt offerings after the flood. God ordered Abraham to offer his son, Isaac, in a burnt offering in Genesis 22, and then provided a ram as a replacement. After suffering through nine of the ten plagues, Pharaoh decided to let the people go from bondage in Egypt, but his refusal to allow the Israelites to take their livestock with them to offer burnt offerings brought about the final plague that led to the Israelites' delivery (Exodus 10:24-29).

The Hebrew word for "burnt offering" actually means to ascend, literally to "go up in smoke." The smoke from the sacrifice ascended to God, "a soothing aroma to the LORD" (Leviticus 1:9). Technically, any offering burned over an altar was a burnt offering, but in more specific terms, a burnt offering was the complete destruction of the animal (except for the hide) in an effort to renew the relationship between the Holy God and sinful man. With the development of the law, God gave the Israelites specific instructions as to the types of burnt offerings and what they symbolised.

According to Law, the priest had to make sure that there was a continuous burnt offering unto the Lord. The burning fires also served as a day and night sweet aroma to the Lord and served as an indication of the people's commitment to serving and worshipping the Great I AM. Just as the burnt offering was a sign of general atonement - a request for a renewed relationship with God – just so we must also be a living burnt offering unto the Lord. It says in Romans 12: 12 *I beseech you therefore, brethren, by the mercies of God, that you present your bodies a living sacrifice, holy, acceptable to God, which is your reasonable service. 2 And do not be conformed to this world, but be transformed by the renewing of your mind, that you may prove what is that good and acceptable and perfect will of God.*

Just as that offering was on the altar, and just as that offering was consumed by fire, so we need to offer ourselves up to the Lord and we need to be consumed by His fire [Holy Spirit/His Glory/His Presence]. But this should be a continuous process where just as the fire on the altar never had to go out [so there always needed to be an offering], just so we need to remain as a constant offering unto God so that His fire may continue to burn and dwell in us. This calls for constant submission, yielding, and abiding in the Lord. To restore to the altar calls for us to constantly behold the Lord and abide in His presence where He becomes all in our lives, all the time.

To keep the fires burning implies being a continuous living sacrifice unto the Lord, so that we may continually be a sweet fragrance unto the Lord. We must continually lift up our lives to the Lord to His Glory and for His Glory. It says in the New Testament that we must not quench the fire of the Holy Spirit (1 Thessalonians 5:19). Now, taking into consideration that according to Romans 12 we must be like a living offering unto the Lord, and if the fire that burns within us is the fire of Holy Spirit, therefore we must be like that offering as in Leviticus 6 where the fire never burns out. Therefore, the Lord says we must be on fire for Him as a burnt offering [living sacrifice], 24 hours a day, and seven days a week!

To keep the fires burning means to restore our commitment to God, to rediscover our passion, our zeal and our loyalty unto Him. And we can only be on a fire for God like the burnt offering in the days of old by allowing the fire of the Holy Spirit to burn and consume us 24 hours a day, seven days a week! We need to constantly be in submission to the Lord and allow Him to consume us so that He may increase and we decrease. By being a continuous offering unto God, we shall make sure the fire keeps burning! Anybody who has ever stoked a fire will know it is hard work. You need to constantly be aware of the fire, and what the fire is doing. Indeed, to feed the fire, you need to fuel it so that it can continue to burn.

We are, as the living sacrifices, the fuel for the Holy Spirit's fire so that the Shekinah flames of God can burn within us, all the time. A fire can only burn when there is fuel, so the Holy Spirit can only burn in us when we are the fuel unto the Lord as a living sacrifice.

We read in 1 Kings 18 how the Prophet Elijah went up the mountain Carmel to challenge the prophets of Baal. Elijah set up an altar to make an offering unto the Lord. And when he prayed, fire fell from heaven and consumed the offering. There can be no fire unless there is an offering! The Holy Spirit cannot burn or consume us unless we are first willing to be a living sacrifice unto the Lord. Our Lord is an all-consuming fire – He needs to consume us all the time. Unless we are willing to first sacrifice ourselves and unless we are willing to first give ourselves unto the Holy Spirit, and unless we are prepared to be a living offering unto God, then the fire from heaven can't fall and the fire of God cannot burn with us. When the Lord, therefore, says that the fire of the burnt offering must keep burning 24 hours a day, it means that WE must therefore be an offering 24 hours a day so that the Lord can continuously burn within us.

But once the fire begins to burn within us, the Lord says then we must continue to be a living offering unto Him so that the fire can continue to burn in our lives. So often we offer ourselves unto God, allowing for the Holy Spirit to burn within us, but then we will become consumed by the world or by the self or even the ways of the devil until the fire within dies. You see, we cannot be consumed by both the Lord and by the world. One is a holy fire, the other is profane. One is light, and the other is darkness.

It says in "1 John 1: 5 This is the message which we have heard from Him and declare to you, that God is light and in Him is no darkness at all. 6 If we say that we have fellowship with Him, and walk in darkness, we lie and do not practice the truth. And also ... 1 John 2: 15 Do not love the world or the things in the world. If anyone loves the world, the love of the Father is not in him. 16 For all that is in the world—the lust of the flesh, the lust of the eyes, and the pride of life—is not of the Father but is of the world. 17 And the world is passing away, and the lust of it; but he who does the will of God abides forever."

We cannot be a burnt offering only for a day or a couple of hours! We can only be a true living burnt offering unto God when we allow His fire to continuously burn within us. But the fire will only continuously burn the more we feed the fire, which means the more we sacrifice ourselves the greater the Presence of God and the greater the sweet aroma! A true disciple after al denies himself and carries his cross. As we thus deny ourselves and live only for God, how that flame will burn and burn!

We need to constantly work at becoming more like the Lord so that the fire can rage deeper and higher within us. God is an all-consuming fire (Hebrews 12:29). This means that God wants to burn and consume us completely and utterly just as the fire consumed the burnt offering of Leviticus 6.

Remember, a burnt offering was the complete destruction of the animal (except for the hide).

God wants to consume us completely but we need to be a living sacrifice who will allow God to consume us completely all day. We need to be completely and utterly submitted to the Lord so that His fire by the Spirit may rage within and so burn away the dross of our sins. Only then will the gold of godliness manifest!

The problem is that we want to live for Him one day and the next day we don't want to live for Him. One day we walk in the light and the next day we are in the darkness.

One day we are doing what He tells us to do and the next day we are not doing what He tells us to do. God has called us to be a living offering where the fire of the Holy Spirit burns indeed 24 hours a day, seven days a week! This means that for 24 hours a day you are under the submission of the Holy Spirit, and you are submitted to the Lord's will and you are allowing for the Holy Spirit to consume you 24 hours a day.

To be a true living offering means living for God 24 hours a day and you are not allowing God's Presence to be tainted. To allow the fires to keep burning, you need to allow yourself to be completely changed in the image of God every day in every way because then we are an offering on fire for the Messiah! We are called to preach the Good News, in accordance to the Great Commission, and to let our light shine (Matthew 5). We are called to walk in God's authority so that we can establish God's Kingdom in the midst of darkness in the hearts of those we are walking in darkness. We therefore cannot walk in darkness and in the next day try to walk in the light. We cannot wander in love and the next moment hate. We cannot wander in the Spirit while living for the flesh. We cannot compromise by serving the world and by serving God. We cannot live for the self and also live for God. We have to be conformed to the image of Jesus. We need to become formed and we need to become more like God every day.

So to keep the fires burning 24 hours a day speaks of the constant work of the Holy Spirit in our lives so that we can become constantly more like God. But what is happening is that we live for God and then we also try to serve the world. This is idolatry. One day the fire on the altar burns bright, and the next minute the fire is dying. We as the living offering must always be on fire for God, and not allow idolatry and the world or the flesh to quench the fire of the Spirit! We cannot be one minute a sweet aroma and the next minute smell like a pile of ashes! We need to decide what we want to do. We are either going to walk in the manifestation of His holiness and righteousness because we have already been made holy by the Blood of Jesus or we must walk in the flesh. To keep the fires burning manifests holiness and righteousness.

This is the great work of the Holy Spirit – burning in us all the time so that we can change in His Presence and become more like Christ. By the inner working of the Spirit, we can always walk in the truth, never compromised, never be deceived and always victorious! It says in "2 Timothy 1: 6 For this reason I remind you to fan into flame the gift of God, which is in you through the laying on of my hands."

We have indeed been given the task to work out our salvation with fear and trembling, meaning we have an obligation and a duty by choice and by the decision to keep fighting the good fight of faith and to keep on walking the narrow road of truth and life. The Holy Spirit has been poured out to aid us, but we need to allow the Spirit to work by giving the Spirit room to operate in our lives. Then the flame within us will be fanned and we can start walking in our spiritual gifts and callings. We as God's priests have an obligation and a duty to keep His flame within us burning through obedience, faithfulness, loyally and dedication unto God. We must never, therefore, quench the fire of the Holy Spirit, for then we quench the operation and function of the Spirit in our lives.

Indeed, these days we are making too many excuses - we are trying to justify everything in terms of why we are not walking in God's glory. We are trying to find a purpose and a reason for why we cannot do things in God's will. God says He is looking at the church and He is looking at His children and He is seeing so many 'offerings' where the fire burns one day and then for a while it is dead – sometimes for months or even years! This cannot be for we must either allow the Holy Spirit to consume us or we are going to allow the devil to consume us. We need to decide, otherwise, we are going to be a burnt offering one day and the next day we are going to be like a pile of ashes. We need to decide what we are going to do, because if we decide to live for God then we need to work out our salvation with fear and trembling.

Matthew 3: 11 "I baptize you with water for repentance. But after me comes one who is more powerful than I, whose sandals I am not worthy to carry. He will baptize you with the Holy Spirit and fire. 12 His winnowing fork is in his hand, and he will clear his threshing floor, gathering his wheat into the barn and burning up the chaff with unquenchable fire." We can only walk in the fire of God [baptism] if we are a true and willing sacrifice. And by that fire of God, the Spirit will cause the old man to die and the new man to be reborn.

Now, consider the following. The coals that were taken from the Altar of Burned Offering served as the coals to be placed on the Altar of Incense. The Altar of Incense served as a symbolic lifting of prayers to the heavens, becoming like a sweet aroma to the Lord. If we want to keep the fires burning, then this means constant prayer (Ephesians 6), constant dedication, constant worship and constantly walking in His ways. Revelation 8:4: And the smoke of the incense, which came with the prayers of the saints, ascended up before God out of the angel's hand.

Coals in the Bible spoke about purification (repentance) but also judgment. In Isaiah 6, the angel of the Lord touched the lips of the prophet to bring forth purification and remittance of sin. Now Isaiah can pray and speak prophetically day and night just as if he had become the Altar of Incense. Isaiah 6: And the foundations of the thresholds shook at the voice of him who called, and the house was filled with smoke. 5And I said: "Woe is me! For I am lost; for I am a man of unclean lips, and I dwell in the midst of a people of unclean lips; for my eyes have seen the King, the LORD of hosts!" 6Then one of the seraphim flew to me, having in his hand a burning coal that he had taken with tongs from the altar. 7And he touched my mouth and said: "Behold, this has touched your lips; your guilt is taken away, and your sin atoned for."

Saints, we must not grow tired of carrying the cross, and we must not grow tired of prayer, worship, dedication, keeping our hearts open to repentance and walking in His Spirit. Now, here is the wonderful thing – when we carry the cross, we are covered by the shadow of Jesus, who shadowed Simon – we are covered by the oil and blood-stained beams of the cross – we are therefore under His covering. As we carry the cross, our backs bend in voluntary submission and worship, we stand UNDER the Covenant of the Blood, as shed on the cross.

In Jeremiah 33 the Lord says He has a covenant with us day and night. By keeping the fires burning and carrying the cross night and day, from early to late, we are honouring the Covenant and come under God's order. Yet, as we carry the cross, we also sacrifice our times, our agendas, our way and ourselves. We come UNDER His will and way and glory.

When we, therefore, keep the fires burning on the altar, meaning we walk day and night under and in His Covenant as living sacrifices, we will therefore also generate coals of fires spiritually to serve as a sweet aroma unto the Lord. By keeping the fires burning, we become a sweet aroma unto the Lord. Still today, the Lord points out how many times do we not grow tired of carrying the cross and how many times do we not let the fires grow cold and how many times do we not shun the light of the Holy Spirit? We need to fan the flame by continually praying. Prayer is our communication with the Father and his communication with us. In order to maintain an active and growing relationship with someone, you must communicate with them. It says in I Thessalonians 5:17(KJV) to pray without ceasing. We need to be in constant fellowship with Him, praying, seeking Him, denying ourselves and walking in His presence.

As we remain a burning sacrifice for the Lord, not allowing the flame of His Glory within us to die, then we shall be a true living sacrifice unto His honour and glory. Let us be alive unto the Lord by burning for Him. For then the fire within will be pure fire, not one which is profane by our immorality and idolatry.

# God's fire exposes the foundation of the counterfeit prophetic

Ephesians 2 declares: "19 Now, therefore, you are no longer strangers and foreigners, but fellow citizens with the saints and members of the household of God, 20 having been BUILT ON THE FOUNDATION OF THE APOSTLES AND PROPHETS, Jesus Christ Himself being the chief cornerstone, 21 in whom the whole building, being fitted together, grows into a holy temple in the Lord, 22 in whom you also are being built together for a dwelling place of God in the Spirit."

The apostles and the prophets have always acted as the mouthpiece of God. They have laid the foundation of God's truth, His Word, His ways and His Kingdom. And still today, contrary to popular belief and assumptions, the apostles and prophets still exist. They do not ADD to the foundation, for the foundation has been laid, but they uphold the foundation, defend it, proclaim it, and reveal its true nature and purpose. They seek not to build for their gain or glory, but to exalt the Builder Himself – Jesus – He who has built as all into the holy priesthood of God. For this reason, we read in "Acts 2: 41 Then those who gladly received his word were baptized; and that day about three thousand souls were added to them. 42 And they continued steadfastly IN THE APOSTLES' DOCTRINE AND FELLOWSHIP, in the breaking of bread, and in prayers."

The apostles' doctrine of Acts 2 is the foundation that has been laid. It is God's truth. It is God's Word that stands forever. No one can destroy such a foundation. You can only build a different one and pretend that it is the true foundation. And this is what happens in the false prophetic movement, where the false prophet is laying a counterfeit foundation of no worth or value. For this reason, we read in "Ezekiel 13: 13 Therefore thus says the Lord God: "I will cause a stormy wind to break forth in My fury; and there shall be a flooding rain in My anger, and great hailstones in fury to consume it. 14 So I will break down the wall you have plastered with untempered mortar, and bring it down to the ground, so that its foundation will be uncovered; it will fall, and you shall be consumed in the midst of it. Then you shall know that I am the Lord. 15 "Thus will I accomplish My wrath on the wall and on those who have plastered it with untempered mortar; and I will say to you, 'The wall is no more, nor those who plastered it, 16 that is, the prophets of Israel who prophesy concerning Jerusalem, and who see visions of peace for her when there is no peace,' " says the Lord God."

Anything that is not built upon God is of no value. It cannot last and its deceptive nature shall be revealed. God likens such deceptive work as 'plastered it with untempered mortar', which means not brought to a proper consistency or hardness. It is, therefore, brittle and will crumble easily. It is weak, destructible and fallible. This is unlike the foundation of God that stands the test of time as revealed in "Matthew 7: 24 Therefore whoever hears these sayings of Mine, and does them, I will liken him to a wise man who built his house on the rock: 25 and the rain descended, the floods came, and the winds blew and beat on that house; and it did not fall, for it was founded on the rock. 26 "But everyone who hears these sayings of Mine, and does not do them, will be like a foolish man who built his house on the sand: 27 and the rain descended, the floods came, and the winds blew and beat on that house; and it fell. And great was its fall."

God's word against the false prophets in Israel was also underlined in "Ezekiel 22: 27 Her princes in her midst are like wolves tearing the prey, to shed blood, to destroy people, and to get dishonest gain. 28 Her prophets plastered them with untempered mortar, seeing false visions, and divining lies for them, saying, 'Thus says the Lord God,' when the Lord had not spoken." Still today, nothing has changed. The false prophetic movement with its lies and deceptions only produces false visions. It holds no value and its foundation is but weak. It causes destruction and division.

In 1 Corinthians 3 we read "2 Now if anyone builds on this foundation with gold, silver, precious stones, wood, hay, straw, 13 each one's work will become clear; for the Day will declare it, because it will be revealed by fire; and the fire will test each one's work, of what sort it is. 14 If anyone's work which he has built on it endures, he will receive a reward. 15 If anyone's work is burned, he will suffer loss; but he himself will be saved, yet so as through fire." Truly, we cannot fool God. He knows who is building on the true Rock of Jesus and who is building with untempered mortar. He knows who is true to the real foundation and who seeks to build another. We may be fooling people, which is happening in churches, but it will not stand against the fire of God. God will always be against false words and visions, which many times are nothing more than divination. It causes people to believe in a false foundation and to build upon such a weak foundation.

Only when we move in God's will, in His Spirit and truth, can we remain standing on the true foundation and uphold it. Anything else is foolishness and dangerous. The false prophetic movement is right now continuing to present a different foundation of truth, and many are embracing it and trusting their lives to it. Yet when the storms come and when the fire of God falls as on Mount Carmel, then such a foundation is found wanting. Just so the work of the Pharisees and Sadducees, who held onto the Law, was found wanting. Jesus said to them in "Matthew 23: 25 "Woe to you, scribes and Pharisees, hypocrites! For you cleanse the outside of the cup and dish, but inside they are full of extortion and self-indulgence. 26 Blind Pharisee, first cleanse the inside of the cup and dish, that the outside of them may be clean also. 27 "Woe to you, scribes and Pharisees, hypocrites! For you are like whitewashed tombs which indeed appear beautiful outwardly, but inside are full of dead men's bones and all uncleanness. 28 Even so you also outwardly appear righteous to men, but inside you are full of hypocrisy and lawlessness."

We read in "Micah 3: Thus says the Lord concerning the prophets who make my people stray; who chant "Peace" While they chew with their teeth, but who prepare war against him who puts nothing into their mouths: 6 "Therefore you shall have night without vision, and you shall have darkness without divination; the sun shall go down on the prophets, and the day shall be dark for them. 7 So the seers shall be ashamed, and the diviners abashed; indeed they shall all cover their lips; for there is no answer from God." God acted harshly against the false prophets in the Old Testament, and He still does today. For those who pretend to be speaking God's Word, or those who pretend through being deceived themselves that they are seeing visions even if God has not spoken, must know that they are playing with fire. God shall not be mocked and He is not fooled. To proclaim a false word – intentionally or unintentionally - is very dangerous, for it breeds deception and upholds not God's foundational truths.

Indeed, the true prophet knows the foundation, adheres to it and declares it. The true prophet does not challenge it or build another one. It is the foundation that has forever existed. Revelation 13:8 declares, "All who dwell on the earth will worship him, whose names have not been written in the Book of Life of the Lamb slain from the foundation of the world." Those who truly follow God follow the Lamb who was slain to uphold the foundation, for He is the foundation! Hebrews 1 declares of Christ: "1 God, who at various times and in various ways spoke in time past to the fathers by the prophets, 2 has in these last days spoken to us by His Son, whom He has appointed heir of all things, through whom also He made the [b]worlds; 3 who being the brightness of His glory and the express image of His person, and upholding all things by the word of His power, when He had [c]by Himself purged our sins, sat down at the right hand of the Majesty on high, 4 having become so much better than the angels, as He has by inheritance obtained a more excellent name than they."

Colossians 1 declares: "17 And He is before all things, and in Him all things consist." Jesus is the Word, and so we read in "John 1: 1 In the beginning was the Word, and the Word was with God, and the Word was God. 2 He was in the beginning with God. 3 All things were made through Him, and without Him nothing was made that was made. 4 In Him was life, and the life was the light of men. 5 and the light shines in the darkness, and the darkness did not comprehend it." He has always been the foundation of our hope and salvation. And so every declared word of the true prophets and apostles have upheld this truth. For this truth sets us free (Matthew 8:32). Any other 'truth' or foundation only deceives, for Jesus is the Rock that will keep standing.

Of Jesus, we read in "Malachi 3: 2 "But who can endure the day of His coming? And who can stand when He appears? For He is like a refiner's fire and like launderers' soap. 3 He will sit as a refiner and a purifier of silver." God is an all-consuming fire. Luke 12:2-3 says, "For there is nothing covered that will not be revealed, nor hidden that will not be known. Therefore whatever you have spoken in the dark will be heard in the light, and what you have spoken in the ear in inner rooms will be proclaimed on the housetops."

We cannot fool God. He knows what is real and false. He knows those who are fooling people and those trying to fool God. Yet God is light. In Him, there is no darkness. He is not deceived. So woe to those who keep on deceiving people with lies and leading people away from the true foundation, for only in Christ is our hope of glory.

Psalm 11 says, "3 If the foundations are destroyed, what can the righteous do?" Indeed, the devil has been busy for a long time trying to break down God's foundation in the church through lies and deceptions. And if we are building or upholding or trusting in a wrong foundation, we are in trouble. We need to discern if we are truly standing on the right foundation and believing and upholding it. The counterfeit prophetic movement has certainly added to such calamities and troubles of confusing and deceiving people to what is the real and true foundation! May we indeed seek the true foundation and not deviate from it!

# Revival fire flowed from the Upper Room

How we need to come alive again in the power of the Holy Spirit to be true representatives of God on this earth! How we need the wind of the Spirit to blow again through our churches, our hearts and our lives!

How we need to again seek the Spirit of God to lead us in all truth, in power, in boldness, in God's beauty and strength! God has spoken prophetically about how the Church needs to get back to the Upper Room. This means we need to reconnect with the Spirit. For directly after the rushing wind, there was revival. And such revival continued and flowed like a mighty river beyond the Upper Room and into the streets of Jerusalem, and still today to the outer reaches of the world. The revival in the Upper Room was sustained and gained momentum, for it was the Holy Spirit that was birthing the church.

In Acts 2, it says that the Lord added to the church daily those who were being saved. Yes, God was in control, thus the Spirit, and not man. To 'add' speaks of divine intervention. Thus pure revival! How we need to yield and submit again to the Lord and just connect with the Spirit of God.

Indeed, how we need the Spirit of God to breathe life into us! How we need the Holy Spirit to shake our worlds so that we become alive from our spiritual apathy to be on fire for God!

We need the Holy Spirit to be filled with conviction and a certainty that God is faithful and true. How we need the holy fire of God to burn in our bones so that the dry bones may live and the spiritually dead and lost and forgotten may be revived.

In Matthew 3, John the Baptist said: "11 I indeed baptize you with water unto repentance, but He who is coming after me is mightier than I, whose sandals I am not worthy to carry. He will baptize you with the Holy Spirit and fire."

Glory to God. How we need the fire of the Spirit in our churches again! For such fire rested like tongues upon the first disciples. And such disciples had no great wealth or influence, yet changed the world. They had a lasting impact because the Spirit of God dwelt within them, radically transforming them into the image of the Kingdom. They were truly on fire for God, infused with the Holy Spirit. Yes, we do not need more programmes or agendas in churches, but we just need the Holy Spirit to lead us as Elijah and Elisha were led in power.

"The purpose of Jesus is not only to save men from their sins, but by the grace of God to begin in the souls of men that marvelous development in the nature and mind and understanding of God our Father, until by the grace of God we are able to take our place and our part in the kingdom of Jesus Christ and bear our share of responsibility." — John G. Lake, Spiritual Hunger, The God-men and Other Sermons

Lake also said that the life of the Christian without the indwelling power of the Spirit in the heart is a weariness to the flesh.

Smith Wigglesworth, the apostle of faith, often used the term "the blast of heaven" to describe the power of the Holy Spirit, particularly the event of Pentecost, which was accompanied by a "mighty rushing wind". The phrase reflects his belief that God's power is still available but that believers can become afraid of it. It is associated with his teachings on radical faith, a deep connection with God, and the necessity of a pure heart for God's power to flow through a person.

He used the phrase to challenge the church, suggesting that they were sometimes frightened of God's raw power rather than embracing it. The concept emphasises that believers must be receptive to the power of the Holy Spirit, which Wigglesworth believed was not limited or exhausted.

His teachings stressed that a "blast of heaven" is dependent on having a pure heart and a deep relationship with God, free from sin and fear. It's not about feeling a certain way, but about a conscious, faith-filled choice to be available to God so His power can operate through you.

Indeed, the church needs to embrace the blast from heaven and the fire that empowers the believer for supernatural living. God has called the church to walk in victory, and not in defeat. We need to be on fire with the Hoyl Spirit!

For Paul wrote in "1 Corinthians 2: 1 And I, brethren, when I came to you, did not come with excellence of speech or of wisdom declaring to you the testimony of God. 2 For I determined not to know anything among you except Jesus Christ and Him crucified. 3 I was with you in weakness, in fear, and in much trembling. 4 And my speech and my preaching were not with persuasive words of [b]human wisdom, but in demonstration of the Spirit and of power, 5 that your faith should not be in the wisdom of men but in the power of God."

Paul, on the Road to Damascus, was reborn when he met Jesus. And from that day, he moved in the power of the Holy Spirit (Acts 1:8), fulfilling the Great Commission by declaring the Good News far and wide. Revival truly followed Paul, for Paul was following Christ in Spirit and truth. Paul had crucified his flesh and was now regenerated by the Spirit of God. For the water of life inside of him was manifesting wherever Paul ministered by the grace and power of God.

It says in Mark 16 that signs and wonders follow those who believe in Christ. Yes, revival must follow the disciple, for the disciple follows the author of life! For as we follow Christ, we walk in His life and Spirit, and by such life and Spirit, the lost shall know that God still redeems and saves the broken, the lost and the forgotten!

We need to remember no one else can save us. God sent Jesus, His one and only Son, to earth so that He could make a way for our salvation (John 3:16). After living a perfect life, Jesus was crucified, bearing the punishment for our sins upon Himself. He was resurrected from the dead three days later, conquering death. When we place our faith in Jesus and His sacrifice, we are saved and filled with the Holy Spirit. The Holy Spirit within us is what enables us to live out the spiritual rebirth that has taken place: "But I say, walk by the Spirit, and you will not gratify the desires of the flesh" (Galatians 5:16). Yet it is also the Spirit that wakens us up from our slumber through divine conviction. Those legitimately born again are indwelt by the Holy Spirit (John 3:5). What does it mean to have the Holy Spirit living within us? Fundamentally, it means that the Holy Spirit is communicating a conviction about Christ's moral beauty to the eyes and ears of our hearts.

We need to understand very clearly that it is by the Spirit of God that we are ultimately made alive to be united with Christ. John 6:63 says: "It is the Spirit who gives life; the flesh is no help at all." So the new birth — and the new life that comes with it — is the work of the Holy Spirit. The Holy Spirit is our direct connection to God and enables us to remain free from the power of sin. When we are spiritually reborn, we walk anew with the Holy Spirit as our guide and companion (John 6:63; Romans 8:14). The Spirit's presence in our life is the seal of our salvation (Ephesians 1:13–14).

Through Christ's sacrifice and the continual presence of the Holy Spirit within us, we can walk with God in the freedom that comes from spiritual rebirth. It is written in Romans 6: (New King James Version): 11 Likewise you also, reckon yourselves to be dead indeed to sin, but alive to God in Christ Jesus our Lord." As our physical life comes from our parents, so life has to come from our spiritual Father – as we are birthed miraculously in the physical, so is our spiritual birth a miracle and one that will forever astound and amaze.

You can also call the Spirit's work a process of regeneration. Another word for regeneration is "rebirth," from which we get the concept of being "born again." Again, the classic proof text for this can be found in John's gospel: "I tell you the truth, no one can see the kingdom of God unless he is born again" (John 3:3). We need to understand that the Holy Spirit, who is God Himself as part of the Trinity, is the source of new life. Moses told the Israelites before entering the Promised Land that "The Lord your God will circumcise your hearts and the hearts of your descendants, so that you may love him with all your heart and with all your soul, and live" (Deuteronomy 30:6). This circumcision of the heart is the work of God's Spirit and can be accomplished only by Him.

Right in the beginning, the world was dark and void of life. We read that the Holy Spirit hovered. Yes, He was first mentioned as part of the Trinity. Only when the Father spoke, "let there be light", did the Holy Spirit move and bring about life. Yes, the Father spoke, and so the Spirit was activated to bring about life, and so the earth was rebirthed. If we are talking about the Holy Spirit being the conceiver of life, consider "Matthew 1:20 But while he thought on these things, behold, the angel of the Lord appeared unto him in a dream, saying, Joseph, thou son of David, fear not to take unto thee Mary thy wife: for that which is conceived in her is of the Holy Ghost." Yes, the Lord Jesus was conceived and brought to life by the Spirit of the living Lord! Indeed, Jesus said He is the Life and He gives Life in abundance, but remember the Lord is ONE, and so Jesus, while on earth, was operating and functioning in the life-giving power of the Holy Spirit! After all, Jesus was baptised by the Holy Spirit.

We read of such a conception also in "Luke 1: 29 But when she saw him, she was troubled at his saying, and considered what manner of greeting this was. 30 Then the angel said to her, "Do not be afraid, Mary, for you have found favor with God. 31 And behold, you will conceive in your womb and bring forth a Son, and shall call His name

Jesus. 32 He will be great, and will be called the Son of the Highest; and the Lord God will give Him the throne of His father David. 33 And He will reign over the house of Jacob forever, and of His kingdom there will be no end." 34 Then Mary said to the angel, "How can this be, since I do not know a man?" 35 And the angel answered and said to her, "The Holy Spirit will come upon you, and the power of the Highest will overshadow you; therefore, also, that Holy One who is to be born will be called the Son of God."

How we need the church to be overshadowed again by the Spirit of God. How we need the Holy Spirit to conceive divine life within the believer and the church in such perilous times. How we need the Spirit of God to set our hearts on fire for God and the lost!

In Luke 1, we read, "41 And it happened, when Elizabeth heard the greeting of Mary, that the babe leaped in her womb; and Elizabeth was filled with the Holy Spirit." There is such beauty where the Spirit is present at the conception of our rebirth. And we need to tell the world of Jesus so that all may know the beauty of such conception. By the Spirit of God, we are reborn and brought to life to the glory of God.

# Consuming fire:
# activated and mobilised

So why is the Upper Room so important? Simple. In the upper room, the church – consisting of Spirit-filled disciples - was ACTIVATED in Power and then MOBILISED to be witnesses unto the ends of the world, thus to fulfil the Great Commission. Yes, the Church was mobilised, for the Church was the disciples, and the Church today is still the living and breathing disciples!

The Upper Room, as the building and the room, was not the Church, but only served as the Ark that housed for a season and a time the disciples who were about to be ignited with fire by the Ruach Elohim! The true Church left the building to be the Church, for they were activated and empowered to be mobilised. In this process of moving forward, they were activated in serving the Kingdom.

Yes, they left the Upper Room! They did not call people to join them in the building, but the Church went into the crowd to bring Jesus to a world dying and in need of a true Saviour! They were burning for God and went into the world to see the hearts of the lost on fire for Christ. The first sermon touched the lives of 3000 people, simply because the disciples were now moving in Kingdom power, and they were focused only upon Jesus and His Kingdom and the lost who needed the King of kings! The disciples were equipped and trained one last time, then activated and then they went. They FOLLOWED first and then out of the door of the Upper Room into the world (literally among the crowd) to preach and teach.

The Church went from that Upper Room – yes, they left what was comfortable and safe – and they embraced a hostile world with the Good News of hope and glory!

Mark 16: 15 And He said to them, "Go into all the world and preach the gospel to every creature. 16 He who believes and is baptized will be saved; but he who does not believe will be condemned. 17 And these signs will follow those who believe: In My name they will cast out demons; they will speak with new tongues; 18 they will take up serpents; and if they drink anything deadly, it will by no means hurt them; they will lay hands on the sick, and they will recover."

Glory to God! The disciples, as the Church, was now activated and mobilised, and yes, signs and wonders of God's power followed them! These disciples were not running after the signs and wonders, but they walked in the Truth of God, filled by the Spirit, and so as they went, mobilised, the Kingdom of God manifested in the world. The disciples were on fire for the Lord, for they understood they were called to be the Church and they were called to be the fulfilment of Mark 16 and Matthew 28. In Acts 3 we read how a lame man was healed, and in Acts 2 we read in verse 43 how "many wonders and signs were done through the apostles" and how the "Lord added to the church daily those who were being saved."

Was God's intention to fill a building when it says adding to the church? No, he was adding followers to the disciples who were willing to preach and teach the Kingdom, thus those who were willing to be also empowered and mobilised!

Suddenly, the living Church was growing for God is a God of Life, and suddenly the Church was truly alive with hope, expectation, and with purpose and intent! The disciples were following the blueprint of Jesus of making disciples, and so the Church, activated and mobilised, was now making a huge impact in the world. Why? Not because of clever sermons, or interesting services or because of the coffee and cake, no, because they were following Jesus in the Spirit of the Living

God, and they were not willing to back down, to be slowed down or to compromise. The active Church was empowered to be a powerful testimony of God's grace and mercy!

They were endowed with power from on High. They were in the fire for God.

So when the Lord speaks of returning to the Upper Room, this is a time for the Church to again be ACTIVATED (a return to the Spirit, to the Kingdom, to the Truth) for the Church to be mobilised to fulfil the Great Commission! Now is the time to move, to follow God's blueprint of discipleship, and to be again filled with Kingdom purpose and intent! Now is the time to be the active Church, empowered in the fullness of the knowledge of Jesus!

For it is time to follow Jesus and to go as commanded by the Lord! Yes, in the Upper Room was the activation and the mobilisation by the Spirit, just as Jesus was activated by the Spirit and then mobilised for three years in His ministry! How we need as the Church of Spirit-filled disciples to be reactivated to go into this world preaching and teaching only the Truth of God and nothing else, for only the Truth of God sets man free in the liberty of the grace of a living God.

We need to return to the 'Upper Room', meaning reconnecting with God, His Spirit, His Son, His Word, His Way, His Will, His Path and His Kingdom, for we are stumbling in the dark of religion.

Are we still burning for God? Fire fell in the Upper Room. The fire falls where an offering has been placed on the altar. The fire is present where the Spirit of the Living God moves in power.

The phrase "God is an all-consuming fire" comes primarily from Hebrews 12:29, which quotes Deuteronomy 4:24. It is a powerful metaphor that appears in several places in Scripture. Fire symbolises purity. Just as fire burns away impurities in metal, God's holiness exposes and burns away everything that is unholy or sinful. God is perfectly holy—nothing impure can remain in His presence.

In the Bible, fire is often associated with God's judgment. When God is described as an "all-consuming fire," it speaks of His power to destroy wickedness, idolatry, and anything that opposes His will. Not because God is destructive, but because sin cannot survive where He is.

For His children, God's fire is not destructive—it is refining. "He will sit as a refiner and purifier of silver." — Malachi 3:3. His fire purifies attitudes, motives, desires and character. Just like gold becomes purer in fire, believers become more like Christ through God's refining work.

In Exodus, when God met Moses on Mount Sinai, the mountain was covered in fire. It showed His majesty, power, and unapproachable glory. You don't stand casually before a consuming fire. After all, God is holy, powerful, pure, and His presence exposes and burns away sin.

For those who reject Him, His fire brings judgment. For those who love Him, His fire brings transformation and refinement. We need to burn again for God! We need to burn in His power to be mobilised and activated to fulfil the Great Commission.

In Luke 24, we find two disciples walking from Jerusalem to Emmaus after the crucifixion. They are discouraged, confused, and disappointed.

Jesus joins them, but they don't recognise Him. He explains the Scriptures concerning Himself. When He finally reveals Himself, He disappears, and they say: "Were not our hearts burning within us as He spoke to us on the road?"

Jesus opened the Scriptures to them. Their hearts burned—not from emotion, but from revelation. The fire came when Jesus explained the Word. The fire of God burns where the Word of God is understood.

The moment their eyes were opened, they ran back to Jerusalem to testify. A burning heart becomes a witnessing mouth.

Paul was on the Road to Damascus (Acts 9) when he met the Lord. Paul was, at the time, zealous without revelation, convinced he was serving God, and spiritually blind. Jesus confronts him with blazing light—a consuming fire—and Paul falls to the ground.

Where the disciples' hearts burned with revelation, Paul's fire was confrontation and correction. Fire refines the willing, but confronts the rebellious. Paul had to lose his physical sight to gain spiritual sight.

The Lord needs to open our eyes again to His Glory and Truth, for sometimes God must stop our movement to redirect our purpose. His Word brings understanding, and His Presence brings surrender. A heart on fire for God leads to a testimony, our calling and our mission. Pride only disempowers and suffocates the flame of God. Glory to God, the same fire of God comforts believers and confronts the proud.

How we need to walk with Jesus again! How we need to yield and submit to the Spirit of God. He is the Word, and so our hearts will begin to burn with passion, clarity, and purpose. His fire consumes and transforms us to be more like God.

The fire of God burns away confusion, burns away wrong thinking, and burns in us to reveal Jesus. We need our hearts ignited in such dark times to walk in the Glory of God.

May the Church keep moving forward in the fire of God to see a world spiritually dying set on fire for His love. May the Church keep going in the power of God, so that the world may see the manifestation of His Kingdom, of His Power and the reality of His Glory. May we be consumed by His Presence, so that we are activated and mobilised to pierce the darkness and set the captives free.

# Strange fire in the wilderness

Moses was a prophet who constantly had to deal with the tension of mercy and judgement. Before examining Moses' life, we must understand that mercy and judgment are not opposites in God, but they are attributes that flow from His holiness. At Sinai, God reveals Himself to Moses: "The LORD, the LORD God, merciful and gracious, longsuffering, and abundant in goodness and truth... forgiving iniquity and transgression and sin, and that will by no means clear the guilty." (Exodus 34:6–7)

Notice the dual revelation: Merciful and forgiving, yet not clearing the guilty. This tension defines Moses' entire leadership journey. At the giving of the Law (Exodus 19–20) at Sinai, God descends in fire, the mountain trembles, the people fear and stand afar off, and the Law is given. Sinai establishes divine order. God is holy, and sin has consequences. Moses understood covenant requires obedience. Judgment is not cruelty, but it is the protection of holiness. This lesson Moses had to learn, yet so many others in the camp were more than willing to turn a blind eye to God's judgement. After all, God is a holy God.

Moses stood between a holy God and a rebellious people for 40 years. Tough job. He embodies three roles: lawgiver, intercessor, and executor of judgment. He must uphold God's holiness, plead for God's mercy, and maintain covenant order.

Throughout the wilderness journey, Israel repeatedly rebels. In Numbers 11, people complain, fire of the Lord burns, and Moses intercedes. The fire stops and so mercy follows repentance. In Numbers 13 to 14, we read how Israel refuses to enter Canaan. God declares judgment that the generation will die in the wilderness. This is after forty years of wandering. Moses again intercedes by saying in Numbers 14:19, "Pardon, I beseech thee." God responds in the following verse: "I have pardoned according to thy word." Yet the consequence remains: they will not enter the land. This establishes a principle that forgiveness removes eternal rejection, but not always temporal consequence.

In Numbers 16, Korah challenges Moses' authority. We read, "1 Now Korah the son of Izhar, the son of Kohath, the son of Levi, with Dathan and Abiram the sons of Eliab, and On the son of Peleth, sons of Reuben, took men; 2 and they rose up before Moses with some of the children of Israel, two hundred and fifty leaders of the congregation, representatives of the congregation, men of renown. 3 They gathered together against Moses and Aaron, and said to them, "You take too much upon yourselves, for all the congregation is holy, every one of them, and the Lord is among them. Why then do you exalt yourselves above the assembly of the Lord?"

It then says, "4 So when Moses heard it, he fell on his face; 5 and he spoke to Korah and all his company, saying, "Tomorrow morning the Lord will show who is His and who is holy, and will cause him to come near to Him. That one whom He chooses He will cause to come near to Him. 6 Do this: Take censers, Korah and all your company; 7 put fire in them and put incense in them before the Lord tomorrow, and it shall be that the man whom the Lord chooses is the holy one. You take too much upon yourselves, you sons of Levi!" .... 16 And Moses said to Korah, "Tomorrow, you and all your company be present before the Lord—you and they, as well as Aaron. 17 Let each take his censer and put incense in it, and each of you bring his censer before the Lord, two hundred and fifty censers; both you and Aaron, each with his censer."

18 So every man took his censer, put fire in it, laid incense on it, and stood at the door of the tabernacle of meeting with Moses and Aaron. 19 And Korah gathered all the congregation against them at the door of the tabernacle of meeting. Then the glory of the Lord appeared to all the congregation."

What happened then? "20 And the Lord spoke to Moses and Aaron, saying, 21 "Separate yourselves from among this congregation, that I may consume them in a moment." 22 Then they fell on their faces, and said, "O God, the God of the spirits of all flesh, shall one man sin, and You be angry with all the congregation?" 23 So the Lord spoke to Moses, saying, 24 "Speak to the congregation, saying, 'Get away from the tents of Korah, Dathan, and Abiram.'" Again, we read how Moses intercedes for the people. He was troubled by the judgement that was about to come upon the people because of their rebellion.

Those who rebelled against God were eventually judged, and so the earth opened, and they were swallowed alive. Harsh to us, but again, it is a demonstration of God's holiness. We are again reminded that God is holy and just. What is interesting is that God demonstrated through the censers how the rebellious ones were not, as themselves, pleasing offerings unto God, and the fire they carried was profane fire.

Hebrews 12:29 says, "For our God is a consuming fire." Deuteronomy 4:24 declares, "For the Lord your God is a consuming fire, a jealous God." God's fire is holy, purifying, righteous, and jealous for exclusive worship. God's fire does not destroy the surrendered believer; it purifies and refines. In Acts 2:3–4 we read of the tongues of fire and how the disciples were all filled with the Holy Spirit. The fire of the Holy Spirit brings power (Acts 1:8), produces holiness, ignites boldness, purifies motives, and burns away sin. We burn in God's pure fire when we yield and surrender unto God, allowing ourselves to be led by the Spirit of God.

When we are consumed by God's holy fire, we are Spirit-led, Christ-centred, set apart, passionate for truth. On the other hand, we can also burn with strange fire, which ignites because of sin, iniquity, rebellion, carnality and Idolatry. Leviticus 10:1–2 tells us how Nadab and Abihu offered "unauthorised fire" before the Lord. Strange fire also represents worship not commanded by God, self-made spirituality, emotionalism without obedience, and prideful ministry. God did not accept fire that did not originate from Him.

Romans 1:25 says, "They exchanged the truth of God for a lie, and worshipped and served the creature rather than the Creator." Jeremiah 2:13 reminds us that broken cisterns hold no water. Idolatry is false fire because it creates passion without purity, zeal without truth, emotion without surrender, and religion without relationship. Anything that consumes your heart more than God becomes an altar. This includes power, ministry status, money, politics, self-image, and even spiritual experiences. False fire excites the flesh, yet holy fire crucifies it.

Pure fire produces humility, repentance, it brings conviction, and leads to surrender. False fire produces pride, it justifies sin, and it becomes detached from the truth, brings confusion and demands self-control. Those in the camp of Moses burned with strange fire. They were full of pride, and they were rebellious. God did not accept their strange fire. 1 Kings 18:24 tells us that the God who answers by fire, He is God. Baal's prophets cried out with no answer, but when Elijah prayed, God sent holy fire from heaven. Baal worship was loud but powerless. God's fire was decisive and consuming. False fire requires performance, yet holy fire responds to surrender.

We must avoid the mistake of Korah. We must be consumed with holy fire. We need to surrender to God so that we may be living sacrifices (Romans 12:1). We need to remove idols (Ezekiel 14:3), for God will not share His glory. As believers, we need to ask the Holy Spirit (Luke 11:13) to burn in us, and we need to stay in the Word (John 17:17).

As a warning, not every intense experience is from God. 2 Corinthians 11:14 tells us that Satan masquerades as an angel of light.

False revival can stir crowds but not produce repentance. Test the fire by seeing if it produce holiness, if it exalts Christ, and if align with Scripture. If not, it is another fire. What are we consumed with? The fire of God or the fire of idols? Holy fire transforms, yet false fire destroys. What burns in my heart? What sits on my altar? What consumes my passion? Because whatever consumes you reveals who you worship. Korah discovered that we cannot mock God with our false and profane fire.

# Spontaneous word: Fire and Power

Fire and power. Glory and fire. Power so awesome. Power so divine. Power so pure. The power that lies not in man. The power that commands universes to exist. A power that commands nations to bow. A power that commands stars to be born, for rivers to flow, for mountains to rise, for clay to become man, for planets to shake and for angels to worship.

Such is the power of the Lord. Such is the power of the One who remains true and who is worthy to be called God above all things. Such is the one who is worthy to be glorified and who is worthy to be exalted. Such is the One, for He is the highly exalted One. Power and fire. Glory and power. Divinity flowing. Tendrils of existence.

By His breath, all flows into being and existence. By His mighty right hand, all things are sustained. Do we not realise? Do we not understand? Shall we comprehend who we serve? Shall we not be fearful and tremble and quake in His might and His power? For dust rises from nothing, and sinews and flesh and bone come together. Blood runs in the veins. Blood brings life. Such is this power. It is all done in a place, dimension and space where time does not exist. It is done. He commands, and it is done. He speaks, and everything quakes in fear and reverence. From His mouth comes the double-edged sword. In His eyes are burning mighty storms of fire. His hand holds all that is and all that was and all that will be. Our God is so powerful, so majestic, so beautiful, and so glorious. Yes, this God, this divine being of such scope beyond earthly understanding, this mighty one loves and heals and makes whole!

Yes, Him, this mighty one, this glorious one, this faithful one, this sparkling one, this divine one of such beauty and awesome splendour, yes, this one loves and heals and is faithful! He who is above all. He who is everything. He who is the reason for all – this one, this beautiful one, this majestic one, this incredible one, this one of such breadth and depth, this one of such fortitude and desire – yes, this one loves us so deeply and he calls us his sons and daughters! Glory, this one, this God of love and wrath, of peace and war, of power and grace, of death and life, this one who has been rejected and despised, who has been worshipped and revered, this one who sits on his throne to be worshipped, this one loves us and calls us His sons and daughters! Can you not grasp how great He is? Is this so difficult? Why turn your heart away? Why flee? Why run? Why hide? "I have always been here," cries the Lord! "Always and always I gave you breath and life and hope and dreams. I love you. I am love! I AM ALL!"

Believer, be calm and still. Take a breath. Feel the blood in your veins. That blood comes from the Lord. Feel the wind on your face. It comes from the Lord. Your breath, your family, everything – it is HIM! Oh, glorious one, be praised and be worshipped. Be exalted and be glorified. Be so praised. Be so worshipped. Be so raised on high. For you who we have mocked and rejected and slandered and ridiculed, You are the one who is the very reason for all, and You uphold all by Your hand. You are the reason that we sing and dance and rejoice. You are the reason. Shall You not be worshipped? Be praised and be glorified? May God be enthroned in thy entire splendour and be our peace. Yes, Lord, be our God and dwell again among us, my Lord. Let all things that are and were and to exist know that You are the ONE who shall be worshipped and adored!

Yes, cry to Him, all universe, cry to Him and bring Him glory! Sing with all the angels. Sing with all your might for He is the glorious one and He shall be praised! Feel that stillness and that power and that glory. Feel it. Sing in angelic tongues. Sing with might and glory. For He is God and King. So it is and was and will be forever.

# A pure temple consumed
# with pure holy fire

If we want to be on fire for God, we have to consider "1 Corinthians 3:16 Don't you know that you yourselves are God's temple and that God's Spirit dwells in your midst?" In the Old Testament, God first dwelt in the Tent of Meeting during the days of Moses, and then in the Temple following the reign of Solomon. With both the tent and the temple, absolutely great care needed to be taken for the 'dwelling place' to be constantly kept sacred, consecrated and undefiled.

Even the utensils used had to be kept sanctified to maintain high levels of consecration. God is a holy God, and with God nothing is impure. God dwelled in such dwellings, specifically in the Holy of Holies, and thus demanded an 'environment' that is completely and utterly kept ALL THE TIME from any form of defilement or corruption. So God moved from Mount Sinai to the tent to the temple. And then He moved by the Blood of the Lamb and the presence of the Spirit into the hearts of man. We are now the temples that accommodate God and where God dwells!

Some may view all the laws and regulations regarding the sanctification and consecration of such dwellings as being legalistic, laborious and archaic. The reality is that nothing was ever done in the Old Testament to be legalistic or religious. It was done with great purpose, intent and functionality. The purpose, in this case, was to show us today that as God required a pure and sanctified dwelling ALL THE TIME, free of defilement and corruption, just so God is looking to dwell in a temple (we as His disciples) that is free of any defilement or corruption. Jesus prayed in John 17:17 "Sanctify them in the truth; your word is truth." As we walk in the truth of God, we walk in His will, in His way, in His Spirit and thus in His holiness and purity. Yes, in such a pure and holy sanctuary, the fire can burn!

Truth keeps us on the right path. The Spirit leads us on such a path of holiness and purity, for the Spirit leads us all in the truth of conviction, spiritual morality and repentance. 1 Peter 1 says, "5 But just as he who called you is holy, so be holy in all you do; 16 for it is written: "Be holy, because I am holy." Thus, the call is for us to be a holy temple in which God can dwell – undefiled, unblemished and uncorrupted by the world and carnality. We are called to be on fire with God, yet such fire burns in the pure of heart and those who are sold out for God.

In Leviticus 22:20 we read how God said that nothing must be offered unto Him with a defect. In Malachi 1:8, the Lord accuses Israel of bringing Him blemished offerings: "'When you bring blind animals for sacrifice, is that not wrong? When you sacrifice crippled or diseased animals, is that not wrong? Try offering them to your governor! Would he be pleased with you? Would he accept you?' says the Lord Almighty." Bringing animal sacrifices to the temple that were blind, disfigured, or sick was a direct violation of the Mosaic Law (Leviticus 22:22; Deuteronomy 15:21). The reason for this command was that such sacrifices dishonoured the Lord. "Do not profane my holy name" (Leviticus 22:32). They were sacrifices in name only; a true sacrifice must cost something, and there was no pain involved in getting rid of something already slated for culling. More importantly, each sacrifice was a symbol of the future sacrifice of Christ, who was "a lamb without blemish or defect" (1 Peter 1:19). The cheap, marred sacrifices of Malachi's time were travesties of Christ's perfection.

The application for Christians today does not involve animal sacrifices, of course, nor is it even directly related to financial offerings. Rather, it is a matter of treating God as holy. Our entire lives must be a testimony of God's perfection, holiness and purity. This concerns all areas of life, ranging from how we speak of God, to how we obey Him and how willing we are to sacrifice our lives unto service. Offering God a blemished animal was like treating God as an afterthought, and it truly mocked Him. We can never treat God in such a manner. He deserves our best and our all. We must be disciples of excellence, seeking to be consumed and be burning all the time with His holy fire. We do this by being an offering of purity and holiness. Thus it says in "Ephesians 5:27 that He might present her to Himself a glorious church, not having spot or wrinkle or any such thing, but that she should be holy and without blemish," and also "Revelation 19:7-8 Let us be glad and rejoice and give Him glory, for the marriage of the Lamb has come, and His wife has made herself ready." And to her, it was granted to be arrayed in fine linen, clean and bright, for the fine linen is the righteous acts of the saints." The message remains clear. As the temple of God, we must remain pure and clean. Be not deflected by the world, and remain an offering aflame with God's presence.

So we need to realise that just as God only dwelt in a tent or a temple that was kept clean, pure and holy, just so God is looking to dwell in a pure, clean and holy vessel. Nothing has changed when it comes to God and the 'environment' He seeks to inhabit. He seeks to habitually dwell with us through the indwelling presence of the Holy Spirit, yet He is looking to dwell in a temple, thus a vessel of blood and flesh, that is consecrated (set apart) and consecrated for God's glory and presence. He is looking for pure vessels in which His fire can burn and burn!

God wants to dwell in us in our entirety. If there is something offensive or defiled or impure or unholy also occupying the 'environment', do we not think this is an affront to the Spirit of God? Everything about us must be completely and utterly surrendered to God. The Lord dwelt in His entirety in the entirety of the tent of meeting and the temple, not in portions. May we truly seek to surrender all to God so that God, as an all-consuming fire, may consume us completely and utterly. For then we become dangerous in love and faith and conduct and speech and thought!

In 2 Chronicles 7, we read of the consecration of the temple. It says, "1 When Solomon finished praying, fire came down from heaven and consumed the burnt offering and the sacrifices, and the glory of the Lord filled the temple. 2 The priests could not enter the temple of the Lord because the glory of the Lord filled it. 3 When all the Israelites saw the fire coming down and the glory of the Lord above the temple, they knelt on the pavement with their faces to the ground, and they worshipped and gave thanks to the Lord, saying, "He is good; his love endures forever." When we truly offer ourselves as a consecrated and pure vessel of habitation to the Lord, then the Lord will fill us with His glory and strength! We shall burn for Him for His fire burns in the sacred and the pure.

The fire was God's approval (just like the fire that came down from heaven to approve of Elijah's offering in 1 Kings 17). It was the fire of cleansing. It was the fire of purification. It was a holy fire, and just so we are called to be vessels of His glory that is on fire in His service. We are called to be consumed by God, and we are called to remain consecrated and sanctified 24 hours a day, just as the fire was not allowed to go out in the ceremonial days of offerings. Indeed, we are now the offering unto God, and we are called to dedicate our lives unto Him – submitted, yielded and surrendered. We are called to yield and submit so that His fire may burn in us all day and every day by the Spirit, so that by the Spirit we remain consecrated, purified, refined, cleansed and a worthy living sacrifice. For in such a dwelling God seeks to inhabit and fill. And such a habitation is a dangerous one full of God's power, glory and might!

During Pentecost, we read at the time of the outpouring of how the tongues of fire rested upon the disciples. The fire was significant, for as in the days of the consecration of the temple, the disciples were now being consecrated and sanctified through the indwelling presence of the Holy Spirit. This is the fulfilment of what John the Baptist said in "Matthew 3: 11 I indeed baptise you with water unto repentance, but He who is coming after me is mightier than I, whose sandals I am not worthy to carry. He will baptize you with the Holy Spirit and fire. 12 His winnowing fan is in His hand, and He will thoroughly clean out His threshing floor, and gather His wheat into the barn; but He will burn up the chaff with unquenchable fire." As the fire fell in the days of Solomon, now it fell in the days of Pentecost. The fire was 'to burn up the chaff' within us as His disciples. Indeed, at Pentecost, the disciples were baptised by the Spirit and the fire. It was the pure fire of holiness, of beauty, of majesty and was intended to consume the disciples. Truly, in the Upper Room, we find that God burned away the old religious ways, and the disciples were not set apart by holy fire in service to God. They were now ready to be pure vessels, thus pure wineskins to receive the new wine of the Holy Spirit.

We also read in 2 Chronicles 7 the following: "11 When Solomon had finished the temple of the Lord and the royal palace, and had succeeded in carrying out all he had in mind to do in the temple of the Lord and in his own palace, 12 the Lord appeared to him at night and said: "I have heard your prayer and have chosen this place for myself as a temple for sacrifices. 13 "When I shut up the heavens so that there is no rain, or command locusts to devour the land or send a plague among my people, 14 if my people, who are called by my name, will humble themselves and pray and seek my face and turn from their wicked ways, then I will hear from heaven, and I will forgive their sin and will heal their land. 15 Now my eyes will be open and my ears attentive to the prayers offered in this place. 16 I have chosen and consecrated this temple so that my Name may be there forever. My eyes and my heart will always be there."

We need to realise that we are now are called to be such a consecrated temple where God dwells. And truly one day we will walk with God side by side. Yet for now, in this earthly body, we can rejoice that as in the days of Solomon, God's eyes and heart will always be with those that God inhabits! Yes, this is a Word from God – a prophetic word – that His heart and eyes are open to His disciples. As God sees, we shall 'see' the Kingdom of God according to John 3. This then connects to Psalm 91 about "1 whoever dwells in the shelter of the Most High will rest in the shadow of the Almighty," and how "the eyes of the LORD are on the righteous, and his ears are attentive to their cry (Psalm 34:15, 1 Peter 3:12), and how "God will never leave or forsake us (Hebrews 13:5)". For this reason we can pray unto God and He will answer. We can rejoice in "1 John 5: 14 This is the confidence we have in approaching God: that if we ask anything according to his will, he hears us. 15 And if we know that he hears us—whatever we ask—we know that we have what we asked of him," and also "John 15:7 If you remain in me and my words remain in you, ask whatever you wish, and it will be done for you."

God thus filled the temple in the days of Solomon and promised to hear them and answer their prayers IF they remain humble, pray, seek His face and turn from their wicked ways. He also promises forgiveness and healing. As the new temples of God, this still applies to us today! We also need to remain humble, we need to continue praying and seeking God, and we need to continually turn from our wicked ways. Thus, the truth of "James 4:7 Therefore submit to God. Resist the devil and he will flee from you." 1 Peter 3:12 also says that God's face is against those who do evil. Matthew 7 declares, "7 Ask and it will be given to you; seek and you will find; knock and the door will be opened to you. 8 For everyone who asks receives; the one who seeks finds; and to the one who knocks, the door will be opened." Glory to God. He forgives when we seek Him and repent. He heals when we cry out to Him. He is still our God of deliverance! In such truth, we are dangerous in our hope and courage!

During the dedication, the Lord said to Solomon: "19 "But if you turn away and forsake the decrees and commands I have given you and go off to serve other gods and worship them, 20 then I will uproot Israel from my land, which I have given them, and will reject this temple I have consecrated for my Name. I will make it a byword and an object of ridicule among all peoples." This warning was fulfilled when both the northern and southern kingdoms of Israel were led away in captivity because of idolatry. Such idolatry was exposed in Ezekiel 8, where the Lord took the prophet into the inner sanctuary and showed him all the abominations that were happening in the temple that was once dedicated and consecrated by Solomon. In this chapter, we read, "17 He said to me, 'Have you seen this, son of man? Is it a trivial matter for the people of Judah to do the detestable things they are doing here? Must they also fill the land with violence and continually arouse my anger? Look at them putting the branch to their nose! 18 Therefore I will deal with them in anger; I will not look on them with pity or spare them. Although they shout in my ears, I will not listen to them." In Ezekiel 10, we read of how the Glory of the Lord departs from the Temple because of the wicked ways of the people.

Also take note 'although they shout in my ears, I will not listen to them." This is in contrast to 2 Chronicles 7, where the Lord said He will hear from heaven, yet He hears those who are truly abiding in God (John 15) and who seek to follow God with a pure heart. Psalm 24 declares, "3 Who may ascend into the hill of the Lord? Or who may stand in His holy place? 4 He who has clean hands and a pure heart, who has not lifted up his soul to an idol, nor sworn deceitfully. 5 He shall receive blessing from the Lord, and righteousness from the God of his salvation. 6 This is Jacob, the generation of those who seek Him, who seek Your face." Glory to God, for this all ties into Matthew 6, which speaks of first seeking God's Kingdom and His righteousness and the rest shall be added. Thus, if we are truly a vessel of purity, we shall seek God's Kingdom and His ways above all. God will hear us, God will keep us, and His countenance will shine on us!

What happened in the days of Ezekiel is still a clear warning for us today. We cannot mock God. We cannot flirt with the world or entertain demons or continue in our old ways of carnality while serving God. We cannot, therefore, be a temple of God that is defiled and corrupted. God will indeed be with us, and hear us, and move powerfully in us to His glory if we keep ourselves from defilement, corruption and spiritual pollution. For then we become dangerous to His Kingdom, we are dangerous in our purity, and in such purity, God dwells in great power and glory! We will then be truly on fire for God, always burning, always yearning for His presence and glory!

As we deny ourselves, we then become a sweet aroma unto the Lord. This is what the Lord is looking for and seeking – for us to be a pleasing offering unto Him. 2 Corinthians 2 (AMP) says "15For we are the sweet fragrance of Christ [which exhales] unto God, [discernible alike] among those who are being saved and among those who are perishing: 16To the latter it is an aroma [wafted] from death to death [a fatal odor, the smell of doom]; to the former it is an aroma from life to life [a vital fragrance, living and fresh]. And who is qualified (fit and sufficient) for these things? [Who is able for such a ministry? We?] 17For we are not, like so many, [like hucksters making a trade of] peddling God's Word [shortchanging and adulterating the divine message]; but like [men] of sincerity and the purest motive, as [commissioned and sent] by God, we speak [His message] in Christ (the Messiah), in the [very] sight and presence of God."

Yes, Lord, may we burn for you! May we be a sweet aroma unto You! Yes, Lord, burn in us. May we be a pre vessel to Your honour, always on fire, always yearning, always seeking Your ways and truth. May we burn with truth, love and desire intimacy with God! Oh God, let Your fire burn!

# Spontaneous word: Fire from Heaven

Fire burning bright, falling from heaven, tumbling and roaring, scorching and piercing. The fire, oh the fire from heaven, so alive, so bright, so majestic, so wonderful, for it tumbles, it roars, it gains momentum, pouring forth into every heart and every soul and every spirit of every son and daughter.

It fills and fills. It expands and roars, cleansing, burning and cleansing. Oh, the fire from heaven, so glorious, so majestic, so powerful, so awesome, so pure. It is fast and so glorious. It just comes and comes – from the throne room, all the way from the Father, all the way from His heart, all the way from His eyes. He stands tall and beautiful, and He speaks, He roars, His hand is extended, and when He speaks that fire, that glorious fire, explodes from within depths and heights unimaginable and unrecognisable.

It explodes and it is so hot, so intense, and so pure. It is the fire of purity. It is the fire of power. Swirling and swirling. It tears and rends and brings forth all that the Father calls. It is alive. It burns. It roars. It fills hearts and minds and souls and spirits. It swirls around the heavens. Oh, it cleanses. It purifies. This fire. This fire from heaven. Glory unto glory. Open wide, heavenly gates. Open wide your heart for the fire from heaven.

Open wide, oh earth. Open wide all that breath. Let it fall. Let it burn. No resistance. Let it fall. Oh, the glory falls and burns. Alive, so alive. Open wide. Hear the angels cry. Hear them sing. They glorify

Him. He is on the throne. He is glorious and majestic. He who is the fire. Beautiful, majestic, and so powerful. Let the fire flow. Glory unto glory. For behold, He is God. He is I AM. Let the fire embrace.

# Fire of Purity

Malachi 3:2 "But who can endure the day of His coming? And who can stand when He appears? For He is like a refiner's fire and like launderers' soap.

Our God wants His children to walk in His purity and holiness. This truth is reflected in the words of Malachi, who was a prophet who lived approximately 400 years before Jesus walked this earth. He was a messenger sent by God to declare certain truths to Israel on behalf of God. Malachi reminded the Israelites of their covenant with God, God's deep love for them, and called them to return to right standing with God.

What the prophet Malachi delivered by comparing God's influence to a refiner's fire was a powerful picture of what happens when God's people encounter his transformative power. We learn from this passage and other Scriptures that part of God's role in our lives is to refine us, just as a refiner would refine precious metals like gold or silver. God knows our sins and our need for cleansing. We are precious to the Lord and for those of us who surrender to Him, He will purify us.

In the third chapter of the book of Malachi, where we find this verse about the refiner's fire, Malachi wrote that the people of Israel had broken their covenant through injustice. The Israelites had accused God of being unjust and absent (see Malachi 2:17). God's response was that he will come to his temple with judgment and refine them. He is not an absent God, but one who is present and hears the cries of his people. God wants to restore us. He wants us to walk in His fire to be cleansed and purified.

A refiner's fire melts down a metal, such as gold or silver, for purification purposes. Once a metal is in its melted state, the dross in the metal rises to the top and is then removed from the metal before it cools. God spoke this analogy through the prophet Malachi to describe how he purifies our hearts. Just as a refiner's fire, God will draw out our dross – our broken, sinful ways – so that we will stand pure and righteous before him. A refiner's fire does not destroy the metal, rather it allows the junk within to come up so that it can be removed. A refiner's fire does not consume, it makes the metal better and more valuable. This comparison helps make sense of what God's redemptive work may look like and accomplish in each of us.

God will purify us in similar ways. He does not consume us to destroy us, rather, being in a relationship with God draws us to righteousness and away from sinfulness. God uses our suffering, our sinfulness, and our shortcomings to refine us just as a refiner's fire, so that the dross within our hearts will rise to the surface and can then be removed. How humbling to stand before God with hearts made pure. This is also illustrated in "John 15: 5 "I am the vine, you are the branches. He who abides in Me, and I in him, bears much fruit; for without Me you can do nothing. 6 If anyone does not abide in Me, he is cast out as a branch and is withered; and they gather them and throw them into the fire, and they are burned. 7 If you abide in Me, and My words abide in you, you[b] will ask what you desire, and it shall be done for you. 8 By this My Father is glorified, that you bear much fruit; so you will be My disciples."

This is the time more than ever for the truth of John the Baptist's words in "Luke 3:16-18: John answered them all, 'I baptize you with water. But one who is more powerful than I will come, the straps of whose sandals I am not worthy to untie. He will baptize you with the Holy Spirit and fire. 17 His winnowing fork is in his hand to clear his threshing floor and to gather the wheat into his barn, but he will burn up the chaff with unquenchable fire." Jesus is truly the refiner's fire! God is an all-consuming fire! For too long, we have mocked Him, twisted His Truth, and for too long, we have built our golden calves. It is now time to know who this God is - He is the I AM in the burning bush, the one who shook Mount Sinai, the one who shook Egypt and the one who has brought down every kingdom and empire that has stood against Him. He is the purifier by fire!

There is indeed a mighty stirring of the Lord in the world. He will bring down strongholds. He will interrupt people's lives. He will restore His order and truth in His Bride. And for those who yield to Him will truly walk in His mighty glory and power. He is looking for a Bride of purity, refined by the fire, for then we shall ascend the hill of the Lord (Psalm 24). Truly, this is the time of "Mark 16: 15 He said to them, "Go into all the world and preach the gospel to all creation. 16 Whoever believes and is baptized will be saved, but whoever does not believe will be condemned. 17 And these signs will accompany those who believe: In my name they will drive out demons; they will speak in new tongues; 18 they will pick up snakes with their hands; and when they drink deadly poison, it will not hurt them at all; they will place their hands on sick people, and they will get well." A Bride refined by purity walks by the power of God and manifests His glory!

The concept of being refined is also seen elsewhere in the Bible. This repeated imagery within Scripture encourages us and reminds us of God's deep love for humanity, which is shown through his desire that we have pure and transformed hearts. Righteousness is vital in the life of believers, and it is not something we can achieve on our own because we are sinful and broken. But by God's transforming love working in us, righteousness is possible. We read in:

Isaiah 48:10: "Behold, I have refined you, but not as silver; I have tested you in the furnace of affliction."

Psalms 66: 10 For You, O God, have tested us; You have refined us as silver is refined.

1 Peter 1:7 that the genuineness of your faith, being much more precious than gold that perishes, though it is tested by fire, may be found to praise, honor, and glory at the revelation of Jesus Christ,

In all of these instances within Scripture that mention being refined, we see common truth relayed: that God refines us for a purpose and to make us more righteous, that God cares about the state of our hearts, and that we are refined so that our faith may be made complete. Malachi's words in this verse echo the never-ending mercy of God. We are not left in our own sin. We are not left to save ourselves. God cares about the condition of your hearts. God comes and meets us where we are and makes us pure, righteous, and spares us the pain of separation from Him when we turn our hearts toward him. And in His embrace by His fire, we are transformed, renewed and edified to serve Him and His glory!

When we need his redemptive work or the refiner's fire, God will come. He will come to each of us and refine us so that we can be set free from bondage and strongholds, and the junk will be removed. God is faithful, and throughout Scripture, we see a consistent message that He cares for his children and will allow us to go through trials and hardships – what we can consider the refiner's fire – to ensure that we will be in right standing with him.

Zechariah 13:9 says, "9 I will bring the one-third through the fire, will refine them as silver is refined, and test them as gold is tested. They will call on My name, and I will answer them. I will say, 'This is My people'; and each one will say, 'The Lord is my God.' " Yes, God desires a pure and holy Bride! He desires for us to be refined so that we shine in His Glory! Jesus said in Matthew 5, "16 Let your light so shine before men, that they may see your good works and glorify your Father in heaven." Our light can only truly shine so strongly and true when it flows from a place of purity and holiness, therefore, from a place of no defilement. As we allow God to refine and renew us like new wine in new wineskins, the light of Christ will shine bright and true in a world surrounded by so much darkness and evil.

Yet we need to allow for the fire to work, which calls for yielding and submitting to the Holy Spirit. When we think of the Spirit of God illuminating and bringing to light what is in the dark or hidden, we think of a lampstand. There are several references to lampstands (sometimes called candlesticks) in both Old and New Testaments that are, in fact metaphorical: the lampstand in John's heavenly vision (Revelation 4:5), the lampstand in Moses tabernacle (Exodus 25:31-40) and Zechariah's fifth vision (Zechariah. 4:2). These three occurrences symbolize the fullness of the Holy Spirit: the seven Spirits of God referenced in Isaiah 11:2: The Spirit of the Lord, the Spirit of wisdom and understanding, the Spirit of counsel and might, the Spirit of knowledge, and the fear of the Lord (Isaiah 11:2). Thus, so often the Spirit is likened to being an illuminating light, for by such light we are examined and the Lord reveals and brings to light what must be brought to light. After all, anything that is hidden or undisclosed or that is hiding in the shadows might only destroy us like cancer.

In Zechariah's vision, God gave Zechariah a vision of the golden lampstand meant to stand in the temple. The meaning of the vision was to show how Zerubbabel would accomplish the overwhelming work of rebuilding the temple by the Spirit of God. The lampstand that God showed Zechariah represented the full ministry of the Holy Spirit. God wanted to assure Zerubbabel (via Zechariah) that the Holy Spirit would continually supply his needs as he embarked on the enormous building project. Thus, we are reminded that it is by God's strength and might that we can be victorious in Christ, and not in our power. We must similarly not just rely on our intellect or wisdom when it comes to continually guarding our ways and keeping the path of the Lord. We need the illuminating light and work of the Holy Spirit; therefore, we need God's fire to burn in us. For it is truly not in our power or might that we overcome or stay grounded and rooted in God, but in the power from on high (Acts 1:8).

In Exodus 25, God gives detailed instructions about the golden lampstand to be placed in the tabernacle the Israelites were building. The lampstand was to be made of pure gold (speaking of divinity), hammered out to the perfect accuracy of God's decree (Exodus 25:31). Gold was the most valuable of all metals (Psalm 119:127; 19:10). Gold is often spoken of in terms of being "tested by fire"; the Bible compares the testing of gold with the testing of the church in 1 Peter 1:7. Out of testing, or refining will come the true people of God (see Zechariah 13:7–9; Job 23:10). Those who withstand the "fire" will be purified (see Numbers 31:23). Thus, we need to allow the Holy Spirit to work in us and not to quench the fire of the Spirit of God (1 Thessalonians 5:19). For the fire purifies and refines. For the fire cleanses and restores. For the fire brings forth life. Jesus is our Refiner Fire (Malachi 3:2-3), purifying and pruning us for a godly life to His glory.

After all, God allowed Daniel to be thrown into the lion's den. God allowed Joseph to be sold into slavery by his brothers. God will allow us to go through hardships, but like Daniel and Joseph and many others, God will be there with us and save us. For this is the process of refinement to produce purity and holiness. Going through the refiner's fire is part of God's redemptive work in our lives; it is not something we have to fear, but something we can welcome from our loving Father. For there are two fires says the Lord – the fire of purging for those who come up to the mountain and who seek the Lord. They shall be refined and purified. This fire prunes the branches that are grafted into the vine. There is also the second fire – the one of God's wrath – and this fire is the one of judgment. Woe to those who had until the end hardened their hearts against God and His Son.

Even though this is the time of judgment in the church and on earth, this is also still the time that mercy triumphs over judgment. For those who choose the Lord, no matter how great one's sin or idolatry, they will be soaked in His loving fire, in His Spirit, in the Blood and in His redemptive love. For the Lord is calling us all back home – calling us to embrace Him and to have a loving and intimate relationship with us. It is time to embrace God's redemptive work of purity and refinement.

As mentioned, while indeed we can examine ourselves to make sure we are truly walking in God's will and ways, there is no greater examiner of our heart and mind than God Himself. Only God truly knows the condition of our spirit. Only He knows the state of our body/flesh. He knows what is amiss, out of alignment, what has become stale, what is oppressed or what needs to be revitalised, restored and healed. And so when we yield and submit and surrender to the Holy Spirit, we allow the light and fire of the Spirit to search 'all the inward parts of the belly'. Thus, the Spirit comes to examine, and in His gentle but true ways to convict us of our errors, faults and where we are out of alignment. And this is all to our blessing. For there is a blessing when we are truly in alignment with God, abiding in His strength and rest.

The Spirit of God is the activator of God's Word by divine power, just as the Spirit moved to bring about creation at the word of the Father in Genesis. Thus it says in "Hebrews 4: 12 For the word of God is living and powerful, and sharper than any two-edged sword, piercing even to the division of soul and spirit, and of joints and marrow, and is a discerner of the thoughts and intents of the heart." The Holy Spirit activates the Word so that the Word becomes not just Logos and Rhema. As the Word becomes active in our lives, the Word enlightens our path and helps to discern 'the thoughts and intents of the heart'. This is how the Spirit of God works; thus we need to allow the Spirit to work in us, and we need to allow the Word to settle and to lead us. After all, we are called to be worshippers in spirit and truth, for then we are truly led by the Spirit and the Word as the examiner of our being.

It says in "Psalm 18:28 For You will light my lamp; the Lord my God will enlighten my darkness." Within all of us there is darkness, or some spiritual malady or some soulish distortion, yet the Spirit of God can truly enlighten us so that we truly know and walk the path of God. Thus it says in "Psalm 26:2 Examine me, O Lord, and prove me; Try my mind and my heart." For the sake of the wellness of our spirit and soul, we need God to examine us. This calls for humility, for submission and surrender to the Spirit of God, allowing His fire and light to burn strong and true within us.

May we again be convicted of our sins! How we need the fire of God to burn within us!

# The refiner's fire and the Word of testimony

We live in a world of great deceptions and apostasy. We live in a world where the lines are blurred between the real and the false, between the uncommon and the common and between what is from God and what is from the devil. After all, the devil is a master at counterfeiting the manifested work of the Lord.

We need thus great discernment in such times to draw a dividing line and to determine the will, the truth, the purpose and the path of the Lord. These are not days of ignorance, for ignorance when it comes to the spiritual realm is not bliss but purely dangerous. The reality is we need to be careful to resist or try to fight something which is actually from God, while at the same time be careful that we do not accept or partake in something which is actually from the devil. Thus, discernment is of great importance in such days where we are called as children of God to uphold the truth, to walk in the truth, to declare the truth and defend the truth. It is after all the truth that sets us free (John 8:32), but then we need to know what the truth is to determine the will and the way of God.

A lot of believers are going through tough times, and some are even experiencing tumultuous tribulations and tests, and some are even under constant demonic oppression and attacks. Some believers are struggling to cope, some are struggling to make sense of anything, and some are struggling with illnesses from which they cannot heal. The truth is that we serve a God who is Sovereign, yet also a God who is mysterious in His ways (Job 11:7). Romans 8:28 says: "And we know that in all things God works for the good of those who love him, who have been called according to his purpose." So yes, sometimes in our seasons, even when it seems we are struggling and fighting to survive to keep our heads above water, we need to trust God, be still and know God is with us. But then again, we also need discernment to know when the devil, like a roaring lion, has found a way to devour in our lives.

So, as believers, we need great discernment for ourselves to know in what spiritual season we are in, why things are happening, what is the purpose, what the will of the Lord is and maybe, where applicable, we have allowed the devil legal ground to attack and oppress. At the same time, we also need great discernment to counsel, to advise, to support and help other believers in order to encourage, edify and uplift. Many times we are simply misunderstanding a spiritual season or we are not seeing the purpose of God, or we are mistakenly ignoring the work of the devil. Thus, great discernment is needed in such times.

Isaiah 11:2 says: "And the Spirit of the Lord will rest on Him .... The Spirit of wisdom and understanding." Indeed, we can only walk in discernment by walking in the wisdom of the Lord, lest we are blinded and misguided by our own ideas, by the flesh, and by our perceptions of a situation.

In its simplest definition, discernment is nothing more than the ability to decide between truth and error, right and wrong. Discernment is the process of making careful distinctions in our thinking about truth. In other words, the ability to think with discernment is synonymous with an ability to think biblically. 1 Thessalonians 5:21-22 teaches that it is the responsibility of every Christian to be discerning: "But examine everything carefully; hold fast to that which is good; abstain from every form of evil." The apostle John issues a similar warning when he says, "Do not believe every spirit, but test the spirits to see whether they are from God; because many false prophets have gone out into the world" (1 John 4:1). According to the New Testament, discernment is not optional for the believer-it is required.

The key to living a life in the will of God lies in one's ability to exercise discernment in every area of his or her life. For then we shall know how to abide in the Lord, how to remain in the Truth and to follow His will. For example, failure to distinguish between truth and error, between what is false and real and between God's will and for example one's own will leave the Christian subject to all manner of incorrect behaviour, action and spiritual guidance. It can even lead to an unbiblical mindset, which results in unfruitful and disobedient living- a certain recipe for compromise.

According to Peter, God "has granted to us everything pertaining to life and godliness, through the true knowledge of Him who called us by His own glory and excellence" (2 Peter 1:3). You see, it is through the "true knowledge of Him," that we have been given everything we need to live a Christian life in this fallen world. And how else do we have true knowledge of God but by abiding in God and through the pages of His Word, the Bible? In fact, Peter goes on to say that such knowledge comes through God's granting "to us His precious and magnificent promises" (2 Peter 1:4). Thus, discernment, which is the ability to walk in the truth of God, is indispensable to an uncompromising life. Without it, Christians are at risk of being "tossed here and there by waves, and carried about by every wind of doctrine" (Ephesians 4:14).

When it comes to discernment, consider what kind of advice or counselling one might give if you were talking to the Apostle Paul. According to 2 Corinthians 11, this is a man who suffered all kinds of hardships. He was beaten, imprisoned, slept in the cold, did not have food, and faced constant threats. Most likely, many of us would have told him he had given the devil a foothold in his life to harass and oppress him. Some might say he still had areas of unforgiveness, or he had failed to repent for something. Some might even talk about unhealthy soul ties or the impact of trauma on his life. Yes, we would have given all kinds of advice, but the reality is that sometimes God allows servants of God to go through seasons of trials and testing. And so you need to know that if this is the case, then what is the purpose of such a season, and yes, is it really God's hand, or maybe it is a work of the enemy. Most of us probably would have stumbled in our discernment when it comes to Paul.

It is the same case as Job. We read in chapter 1: Satan Attacks Job's Character: 6 Now there was a day when the sons of God came to present themselves before the Lord, and Satan also came among them. 7 And the Lord said to Satan, "From where do you come?" So Satan answered the Lord and said, "From going to and fro on the earth, and from walking back and forth on it." 8 Then the Lord said to Satan, "Have you [g]considered My servant Job, that there is none like him on the earth, a blameless and upright man, one who fears God and shuns evil?" 9 So Satan answered the Lord and said, "Does Job fear God for nothing? 10 Have You not made a hedge around him, around his household, and around all that he has on every side? You have blessed the work of his hands, and his possessions have increased in the land. 11 But now, stretch out Your hand and touch all that he has, and he will surely curse You to Your face!" 12 And the Lord said to Satan, "Behold, all that he has is in your power; only do not lay a hand on his person." So Satan went out from the presence of the Lord.

Take note, God allowed the devil to have the power to oppress Job, but not all the power, which is for certain, for God still said that the devil was not allowed to lay a hand on Job. Take note of what the devil said: "Have You not made a hedge around him, around his household, and around all that he has on every side?" God's protection was with Job because Job was a blameless and upright man. And so God will indeed protect those who abide in Him and seek His Kingdom. Of course, the friends of Job misunderstood Job's trials and testing completely. They thought he had sinned or had done something wrong, instead of discerning the truth of what God was doing and the season of Job's life. Job also fell into doubt, most likely because of the bad advice and counselling he received, for he also failed eventually to discern his spiritual season.

Yet we read in Job 42 following Job's repentance: "2 Now the Lord blessed the latter days of Job more than his beginning; for he had fourteen thousand sheep, six thousand camels, one thousand yoke of oxen, and one thousand female donkeys. 13 He also had seven sons and three daughters." Glory to God, all things God works for the good of those who love Him.

Take note also of what Job said in chapter 42: "1 Then Job answered the Lord and said: 2 "I know that You can do everything, and that no purpose of Yours can be withheld from You. 3 You asked, 'Who is this who hides counsel without knowledge?' Therefore, I have uttered what I did not understand, Things too wonderful for me, which I did not know." So Job realised he spoke things which he did not understand. For yes, no purpose of God can be withheld from Him. So too we risk speaking things and counselling people or advising people without understanding God's will, His way or truth. This is merely foolishness, and not declaring the wisdom of God. Again, we need the wisdom of the Holy Spirit to discern, to advise, to counsel, to edify and to uplift.

For Paul, the reality of his testing was most likely found in the truth of "Malachi 3:3: He will sit as a refiner and a purifier of silver; He will purify the sons of Levi, and purge them as gold and silver, that they may offer to the Lord an offering in righteousness."

When it comes to the purifier of silver, also consider the following Scriptures:

1 Peter 1: 6 In this you greatly rejoice, though now for a little while, if need be, you have been grieved by various trials, 7 that the genuineness of your faith, being much more precious than gold that

perishes, though it is tested by fire, may be found to praise, honor, and glory at the revelation of Jesus Christ, 8 whom having not seen you love. Though now you do not see Him, yet believing, you rejoice with joy inexpressible and full of glory, 9 receiving the end of your faith—the salvation of your souls.

Zechariah 13: 9 I will bring the one-third through the fire, will refine them as silver is refined, and test them as gold is tested. They will call on My name, and I will answer them. I will say, 'This is My people'; and each one will say, 'The Lord is my God.' "And I will put this third into the fire, and refine them as one refines silver, and test them as gold is tested. They will call upon my name, and I will answer them. I will say, 'They are my people'; and they will say, 'The Lord is my God.'"

Isaiah 48:10 Behold, I have refined you, but not as silver; I have tested you in the furnace of affliction.

Job 23:10 But He knows the way that I take; when He has tested me, I shall come forth as gold.

Proverbs 17:3 The refining pot is for silver and the furnace for gold, But the Lord tests the heart.

Psalm 66:10 For You, O God, have tested us; You have refined us as silver is refined.

Yes, our God is a refiner's fire, and that makes all the difference. A refiner's fire does not destroy indiscriminately like a forest fire. A refiner's fire refines. It purifies. It melts down the bar of silver or gold, separates the impurities that ruin its value, burns them up, and leaves the silver and gold intact. He is like a refiner's fire. Therefore purity and holiness will always be a process of cleansing, and it is not always easy. There will always be a proper "fear and trembling" in the process of becoming pure. He is like fire, and fire is serious. You don't fool around with it.

This is not merely a word of warning, but a tremendous word of hope, for out of the purification comes hope and blessing and restoration. The furnace of affliction in the family of God is always for refinement, never for destruction. It also says in "Hebrews 12:29: For our God is a consuming fire." God wants to consume all things in our life that prevent a true and deep relationship between us and God, for this will produce a life of life, of peace, joy and spiritual strength.

The truth is, as with Paul, many times we actually go through seasons of purification, and this many times is done through the purifying fire of God. And this has nothing to do with the devil, or legal ground, or with disobedience. Sometimes God allows us to go through such seasons for a reason. For Peter is was about how the genuineness of our faith may be found to praise, honour, and glory at the revelation of Jesus Christ.

If we consider fire and a furnace, consider Shadrach, Meshach, and Abed-Nego who were thrown in the furnace for disobeying the decree of King Nebuchadnezzar. Take note, God did not prevent them from being thrown into the fire, but he did protect them from the flames! They were not scorched or burned, but overcame and thrived! God did not protect Daniel from being thrown into the pit with the lions, but He did protect Daniel from being devoured. It says in 2 Corinthians 12:9: And He said to me, "My grace is sufficient for you, for My strength is made perfect in weakness." Therefore most gladly I will rather boast in my infirmities, that the power of Christ may rest upon me.

It says in "1 Peter 5:8: Be sober, be vigilant; because your adversary the devil walks about like a roaring lion, seeking whom he may devour." God will protect us from the devourer if we remain and abide in Him, walking by the Spirit, for then we shall be sober and vigilant of the schemes and the tricks of the devil. To be sober calls for being well balanced and self-disciplined, thus a life dedicated to God, walking in His will and trusting God.

In Psalm 23 we read "4 Even though I walk through the [sunless] valley of the shadow of death, I fear no evil, for You are with me; Your rod [to protect] and Your staff [to guide], they comfort and console me. 5 You prepare a table before me in the presence of my enemies. You have anointed and refreshed my head with oil; my cup overflows." You see, God never kept David from the valley of the shadow of fear (he was persecuted and threatened by Saul and many other adversaries). But God protected the king of Israel. Yes, David was faced with many enemies, but God's grace was sufficient for David to slay Goliath and to prevail against his enemies. Sure, David did bring calamity upon himself for his sins that followed his gaze upon Bathsheba, but David remained true to God and God strengthened David through so many trials. Like the Apostle Paul, David's life was a testimony to the greatness of God despite all the suffering and hardships.

And what about the story of Joseph, who in Genesis 39 was sold as a slave by his brothers and landed up in Egypt? Did this man do anything wrong? Did he sin? No, this was a season that God would use to not only bless Joseph but ultimately bless entire Israel! So we must be careful not to misinterpret God's purposes and plans, for when we step out of His will. We read the following: 2 The Lord was with Joseph, and he was a successful man; and he was in the house of his master the Egyptian. 3 And his master saw that the Lord was with him and that the Lord made all he did [a]to prosper in his hand. 4 So Joseph found favor in his sight, and served him. Then he made him overseer of his house, and all that he had he put under his authority." At first most of us in the shoes of Joseph would have bemoaned our fate and probably groaned with God, yet Joseph was abundantly blessed despite being sold as a slave!

But of course, the devil tried his tricks again and Joseph was falsely accused (the devil is our accuser day and night), and so landed up in prison. Yet again in prison, he found favour with God, because his imprisonment was not the work of the devil but God had a greater purpose in store. We read "verse 21 But the Lord was with Joseph and showed him mercy, and He gave him favor in the sight of the keeper of the prison. 22 And the keeper of the prison committed to Joseph's hand all the prisoners who were in the prison; whatever they did there, it was his doing. 23 The keeper of the prison did not look into anything that was under Joseph's authority, because the Lord was with him; and whatever he did, the Lord made it prosper."

Egypt suffered a horrible famine at the time, yet because Joseph had correctly interpreted God's warnings (even while suffering and in prison), Egypt had properly prepared for the famine by storing grain. And so when Joseph's brothers travelled to Egypt to obtain grain, Joseph revealed his identity and forgave them for what they had done. He then invited his father, Israel, to move the entire family to Egypt. Pharaoh welcomed Joseph's family and gave them the land of Goshen to live in. You see, God had a great plan for Joseph, but it was a season that needed to be discerned and not to be erroneously interpreted.

Isaiah 54:17 declares: "No weapon formed against you shall prosper, and every tongue which rises against you in judgment, You shall condemn. This is the heritage of the servants of the Lord, and their righteousness is from Me," says the Lord.

Take note, it does not say that the weapon would not be forged. Yes, the weapon will be forged, but it will not prosper! It does not say a tongue will not arise, but God shall condemn it. It says in Psalm 91: Surely He shall deliver you from the snare of the fowler and from the perilous pestilence. 4 He shall cover you with His feathers, and under His wings you shall take refuge; His truth shall be your shield and buckler. 5 You shall not be afraid of the terror by night, nor of the arrow that flies by day, 6 Nor of the pestilence that walks in darkness, nor of the destruction that lays waste at noonday. 7 A thousand may fall at your side, and ten thousand at your right hand; but it shall not come near you. 8 Only with your eyes shall you look, and see the reward of the wicked. 9 Because you have made the Lord, who is my refuge, even the Most High, your dwelling place, 10 No evil shall befall you, nor shall any plague come near your dwelling; 11 For He shall give His angels charge over you, to keep you in all your ways.

In Psalm 91 it says that God does not take away the snare completely, but you will be delivered from it. Take note, there will be terror by night, arrows that fly, pestilence in darkness, destruction and many who will fall. This is all part of the reality of life. We are surrounded by evil, wickedness and calamity, and yes, sometimes we find ourselves in the fire, and in the den of lions, and sometimes we have stepped in the snare, and yes, the darkness will be around us, and the terrors will knock on our door, but through it all, God will protect. He does deliver and restore. God is always in control and has a plan! So yes, we will go through things in life where it may seem God abandons us and where we do not understand why we have to endure such trials and testing, but we need to remember God purifies and prunes. His grace is sufficient for us!

But then again, we need discernment to know when it is God's hand at work or when we have allowed the devil, as the devourer, to gain entry into our life through sin, in whatever form or shape. But yes, we need discernment!

John 9: 1 Now as Jesus passed by, He saw a man who was blind from birth. 2 And His disciples asked Him, saying, "Rabbi, who sinned, this man or his parents, that he was born blind?" 3 Jesus answered, "Neither this man nor his parents sinned, but that the works of God should be revealed in him. 4 must work the works of Him who sent Me while it is day; the night is coming when no one can work. 5 As long as I am in the world, I am the light of the world." 6 When He had said these things, He spat on the ground and made clay with the saliva; and He anointed the eyes of the blind man with the clay. 7 And He said to him, "Go, wash in the pool of Siloam" (which is translated, Sent). So he went and washed, and came back seeing.

This man did not suffer because of some generational curse or because he was in the wrong with God in some or other way, but his blindness was just a natural occurrence in life. But God used this opportunity so that "the works of God should be revealed in him". Yes,

God healed him so that the man could hold onto a testimony of healing and how great God is. We must therefore be very careful to declare something is purely demonic or that it is someone's fault, for sometimes there is a season, or a reason so that God's work may be revealed.

It says in "Revelation 12:11: And they overcame him by the blood of the Lamb and by the word of their testimony, and they did not love their lives to the death." So many times in our seasons of fire, purification, testing and trials, it will not only produce holiness, character and faith but also will lead to testimony. And by that testimony, we overcome this world and the schemes of the devil! For in the fire we draw closer to God, and we grow strong in our spiritual conviction. Paul said, based on his sufferings, the following: "2 Corinthians 11: 30 If I must boast, I will boast in the things which concern my infirmity." And also "Galatians 6:14: But God forbid that I should boast except in the cross of our Lord Jesus Christ, by whom the world has been crucified to me, and I to the world." Paul's suffering truly led to a servant of God who was so determined to follow Christ that he would only boast in God! And so Paul ran his race and was poured out like a drink offering.

In Acts 7 we find Stephen declaring the truth of God and God's role as the true King of Israel. We read from verse 54 Now when they heard this [accusation and understood its implication], they were cut to the heart, and they began grinding their teeth [in rage] at him. 55 But he, being full of the Holy Spirit and led by Him, gazed into heaven and saw the glory [the great splendor and majesty] of God, and Jesus standing at the right hand of God; 56 and he said, "Look! I see the heavens opened up [in welcome] and the Son of Man standing at the right hand of God!" 57 But they shouted with loud voices, and covered their ears and together rushed at him [considering him guilty of blasphemy]. 58 Then they drove him out of the city and began stoning him; and the witnesses placed their outer robes at the feet of a young man named Saul.

Stephen was not spared from being stoned to death, but God used this opportunity to declare His majesty for Stephen saw Jesus standing at the right hand of God. Such testimony is a testimony for all Christians since the stoning of Stephen, for we can all now rejoice that Jesus is alive, real, ascended and sits at the right hand of God! His testimony is our testimony of God's greatness, of God's goodness and that we shall indeed be welcomed as good and faithful servants into the eternal Kingdom. Stephen's death was not a victory for the devil, but a triumphant moment of glory for God and all believers!

When the three servants overcome the furnace in Daniel 3 we read from verse 28 Nebuchadnezzar spoke, saying, "Blessed be the God of Shadrach, Meshach, and Abed-Nego, who sent His Angel and delivered His servants who trusted in Him, and they have frustrated the king's word, and yielded their bodies, that they should not serve nor worship any god except their own God! 29 Therefore I make a decree that any people, nation, or language which speaks anything amiss against the God of Shadrach, Meshach, and Abed-Nego shall be cut in pieces, and their houses shall be made an ash heap; because there is no other God who can deliver like this." 30 Then the king promoted Shadrach, Meshach, and Abed-Nego in the province of Babylon.

Yes, testing produced an incredible testimony! This was also the case when Daniel survived the pit and we read in Daniel 6: 25 Then King Darius wrote: To all peoples, nations, and languages that dwell in all the earth: Peace be multiplied to you. 26 I make a decree that in every dominion of my kingdom men must tremble and fear before the God of Daniel. For He is the living God, and steadfast forever; His kingdom is the one which shall not be destroyed, and His dominion shall endure to the end. 27 He delivers and rescues, and He works signs and wonders in heaven and on earth, who has delivered Daniel from the power of the lions. 28 So this Daniel prospered in the reign of Darius and in the reign of Cyrus the Persian.

In Acts 16, Paul was imprisoned (yes he was not spared), but in the prison, God moved mightily. We read, "5 But at midnight Paul and Silas were praying and singing hymns to God, and the prisoners were listening to them. 26 Suddenly there was a great earthquake, so that the foundations of the prison were shaken; and immediately all the doors were opened and everyone's chains were loosed. 27 And the keeper of the prison, awaking from sleep and seeing the prison doors open, supposing the prisoners had fled, drew his sword and was about to kill himself. 28 But Paul called with a loud voice, saying, "Do yourself no harm, for we are all here." 29 Then he called for a light, ran in, and fell down trembling before Paul and Silas. 30 And he brought them out and said, "Sirs, what must I do to be saved?" 31 So they said, "Believe on the Lord Jesus Christ, and you will be saved, you and your household." 32 Then they spoke the word of the Lord to him and to all who were in his house. 33 And he took them the same hour of the night and washed their stripes. And immediately he and all his family were baptized. 34 Now when he had brought them into his house, he set food before them; and he rejoiced, having believed in God with all his household."

Paul praised God in the midst of the proverbial fire, and testimony arose! Yes, because he was faithful to God, who is the refiner's fire, the jailer was saved! What a testimony!

And of course, the greatest story in the history of mankind is the birth of Jesus, His life on earth, His crucifixion, His resurrection and ascension. Jesus was not spared the cross, for He sought only the will of the Father. Yet His sacrifice is the greatest testimony of love for He died to save all of us who are once sinners and so deeply lost without a Saviour. Indeed, the cross and Stephen's testimony bring home the reality of John 3:16: "For God so [greatly] loved and dearly prized the world, that He [even] gave His [One and] only begotten Son, so that whoever believes and trusts in Him [as Savior] shall not perish, but have eternal life.

Regarding the purifying process, the following story is also well-known. It goes as follows (author unknown):

There was a group of women in a Bible Study on the book of Malachi. As they were studying chapter three, they came across verse three, which says: "He will sit as a refiner and purifier of silver." This verse puzzled the women, and they wondered what this statement meant about the character and nature of God.

One of the women offered to find out about the process of refining silver and get back to the group at their next Bible study. That week, this woman called up a silversmith and made an appointment to watch him at work. She didn't mention anything about the reason for her interest or her curiosity about the process of refining silver. As she watched the silversmith, he held a piece of silver over the fire and let it heat up. He explained that in refining silver, one needed to hold the silver in the middle of the fire where the flames were hottest as to burn away all the impurities.

The woman thought about God holding us in such a hot spot- then she thought again about the verse, that he sits as a refiner and purifier of silver. She asked the silversmith if it was true that he had to sit there in front of the fire the whole time the silver was being refined. The man answered "yes," he not only had to sit there holding the silver, but he had to keep his eye on the silver the entire time it was in the fire. If the silver was left even a moment too long in the flames, it would be destroyed. The woman was silent for a moment. Then she asked the silversmith, "How do you know when the silver is fully refined?" He smiled at her and answered, "Oh that's easy. When I see my image in it."

This is the Lord whom we serve – a refiner's fire and a God of great majesty and beauty. We need to remain discerning, be vigilant, be sober and assess the reality and the will of the Lord at all times. May we continue to walk in His will, to His Glory and let us seek Him and His Way above all. Let us move in His Spirit, do as He commands, obey, yield to His Word for then we shall know His Kingdom is one of power! May we submit, surrender and seek Him above all, for no matter our spiritual seasons, may our lives be a testimony of a God who delivers and who redeems. Let us give the devil no foothold as the devourer, but may we abide in the Lord, be refined and be purified so that our Lord and Master may be glorified.

# Fire to stand in the baptism of trials

There has been plenty of talk about whether the baptism of fire is the third kind of baptism following the baptism in water and by the Spirit. The answer is no, for the 'baptism of fire' is merely the process of following the infilling of the Holy Spirit, who leads us to walk more intimately with God. And such a walk requires refinement and purification (see John 15). By the fire, we are bolstered, strengthened and refreshed daily to stand strong for the Kingdom of God.

The baptism of fire has become a topic of debate in churches. John the Baptist said that Jesus will baptise us with the Holy Spirit and with fire (Matthew 3:11), creating the impression that there are two baptisms. The baptism of the Holy Spirit and indwelling fire is both the work and product of Spirit. It is the same process that is continuous like a flame burning in the night. The fire of the Spirit produces the truth, as we are set free to grow and to be empowered in healing, deliverance and sharing the good news. The fire of the Spirit produces suffering by dying to the self and the world, and it promotes an abandonment unto God that allows for greater growth in purity and holiness. Such holiness and purity lead to a greater spiritual plateau, drawing us closer to God, opening the way for us to dwell in the blessed state of spiritual unity and divine love. Thus, there is no additional baptism beyond the water and Spirit, for both such baptisms lead us on the path of surrender and abandonment unto God.

You can say that the fire of the Spirit follows the baptism of the Holy Spirit, for we first have to be prepared, guided, and taught by the Spirit how to submit and surrender. The fire burns when we willingly surrender to God's will to be completely purified by the Spirit of God. This calls for us to open our spirit, soul, and body so that God can examine the deepest recesses of our existence, entering into the deepest chamber of our spirit and soul. Since the fire is the working of the Holy Spirit, you will find a divine working of God's Wisdom, Love and Power to cleanse and renew us. We, therefore, have to move in faith, believing God is working to transform us more in the likeness of His Son.

Baptism by fire is also a worldly phrase commonly used to describe a person who is learning something the hard way through a challenge or difficulty. Therefore, you can say all believers should undergo some sort of 'baptism of fire' as we learn more about God while facing a myriad of temptations, trials, demonic storms and tests in this world. At the same time, you can also say that while we undergo such challenges, we need the fire of God, thus His indwelling presence, to overcome and to be triumphant in Christ. After all, the fire of God is God's presence, one of purity and also one of judgment. The fire is the work of the Spirit that purifies us through His judgment so that we can know and 'see' God, thus understanding and discerning the manifestation of the Kingdom.

In Matthew 16:24, the Lord said: "If anyone desires to come after Me, let him deny himself, and take up his cross, and follow Me." Even in the life of a disciple, there is the crucifixion, where we need to lay down our own lives to follow God. To yield and submit is surely not easy, for it demands sacrifice and a price to pay. It calls for a willing surrender and to place your life on the altar to burn for God. There is the eternal call for us to deny the world and to seek the ways of the Kingdom (1 John 2). Romans 8 says: "13 For if you live according to the flesh you will die; but if by the Spirit you put to death the deeds of the body, you will live. 14 For as many as are led by the Spirit of God, these are sons of God." By the indwelling presence of God, we undergo our baptism of fire to draw closer to God and to become separated from the carnal and the wickedness of this life.

The life of a disciple is a life of mortifying, thus dying to the self to gain the Lord. Discipleship is thus not always just about the euphoric moments. Just ask the first disciples in the Book of Acts, who were threatened and ridiculed. Our lives must be the reality of "Philippians 1:21: For to me, to live is Christ and to die is gain." Yet how many disciples are willing to truly and utterly die to the Self, to the carnality of the world and to the wisdom of the world to live for God alone?

In the wilderness, Jesus faced the devil after 40 days of fasting. It was a time of isolation. A time of testing and tribulation. It was a time of perseverance and character. The devil tempted the Lord to follow fleshly desires and reasoning, yet Jesus stood firm as the Word and the Saviour of the world. Just so, the Israelites endured 40 years in the wilderness, and their loyalty, faithfulness, dedication and commitment to God was severely tested. Yes, they endured their baptism of fire, just as Daniel endured his time of testing in the wilderness of Babylon. And just so, all disciples face their wilderness of trials and temptations, of battling doubt, the flesh, the devil, the world and one's inner demons. In the wilderness, our character is forged, for the wilderness is also a time of separation and a time of cleansing. Paul admonished believers to stand firm (Ephesians 6, Galatians 5:1), and so it doesn't matter if we endure the storms or the good days of blessings; we must remain true to the Lord. The life of the disciple is also one of the wilderness, not just the Promised Land, for in the wilderness we learn to trust, we learn to know who truly quenches our thirst and hunger, and we learn to have faith and to hold onto the Lord even though it would be easier to let go.

In 2 Corinthians 1:8-11, we learn that Paul and his companions suffered such extreme pressure during a particular situation in Asia they "despaired even of life." Scholars aren't sure what event Paul referred to in these verses, but it was a situation so dire Paul believed he and his companions might die. He saw no way out of the life-threatening situation. And indeed, without God's miraculous intervention, they would have. When all human hope was lost God delivered them by His grace through the prayers of the believers (2 Corinthians 1:11). Such is the nature of being a disciple. There might even be moments when we despair even of life, but God is with us, and His strength is more than sufficient. To burn for God is not always about the great and wondrous moments, but is to hold onto the truth, to resist opposition and to stand strong when the onslaughts are great.

In Judas, Jesus experienced betrayal. And just so, as believers of Christ, we also shall suffer betrayal at the hands of those who seem close to us. This is our constant baptism of fire where believers will always face opposition, persecution and hard times. It is the nature of the world and the devil to resist God and His followers. It is the nature of life and the nature of the devil's work. It is the nature of our humanity, yet the question remains what shall we do in such a time of betrayal, and a time of mistrust? The Apostle Paul experienced betrayal throughout his ministry. Such is normative in the life of the believer according to the Bible. So don't be surprised when it happens to you. We all as believers ultimately go through difficult times, yet the fire of God leads us to overcome and to resist, even though when it seems there is no hope.

The key to such victory is complete abandonment in soul and spirit and body before God (complete surrender). When we abandon ourselves, we lay before the cross our rights, ambitions, desires, fears, weaknesses, sin, calling, purposes (our entire life) so that God will completely saturate our body, soul and mind. In abandonment, we allow God to captivate us, allowing God to be our true King, and our desires and ambitions are submitted to God. Abandonment is our white flag of surrender, not wishing to resist God on any level or in any way. With resistance comes rebellion, so we stop fighting God but now work with God. In submission flows God's power as we yield to His will. And in His will, we discover His goodness to stand strong in the baptism of fire as we burn for God!

The continual process of abandonment allows for God's divine fire to consume us, for we are now vessels that are submitted in the hands of the Lord. This fire produces inward suffering since God's fire reveals to us through wisdom, power and love our deeper impurities, longings and failures. It is these impurities and the guilt and shame of our failures that prevent us from engaging in a far more mature and intimate relationship with God. There is, therefore, painful inward suffering that we have to endure when we are seeking the fire, for we are confronted with the deeper evils of our soul, realising that the 'demons of the darkness' in our inner being have to be slain.

The consequences of the fire are to be found in Acts 2:43-47 (following Pentecost). We find in this Scripture how the first disciples, on the Day of Pentecost, received the Baptism of the Holy Spirit and how the fire rested upon them (the Shekinah presence of God). We find the following results: a) favour with man b) living in the fear of God c) gladness of heart d) continuous growth e) lack of nothing f) powerful deeds were done and g) increase in prayer life. This was all possible because of the fire, thus the work of the Spirit, allowing them the wisdom to mortify the deeds of the sinful nature that set love free so that they could die in themselves. It empowered them to stand for the truth and to fulfil the Great Commission. As we draw closer to God, we come closer to the spiritual centre of complete peace and abundance. We walk the highway of divine unity, allowing God to move like a mighty river freely in our very being.

Abandonment, mortification and purification draw us into the deepest chambers of God's throne room! Such a process guides us on our journey to the deep spiritual treasures of God that must be unlocked in our spirit and soul. The fire is, however, not only a one-day process by the Spirit. It is a continuous process of abandonment, mortification, and purification. The suffering that is produced is, therefore, also continuous and painful, as we are constantly being deeply examined and refined by the fire of the Almighty God. To seek the fire is to seek the deeper realms of God, but it also means surrendering to the suffering of carrying the cross and living completely for God. It is painful to completely surrender our desires, ambitions, and pleasures, letting God become divinely united with our spirit and soul. Yet in the surrender is the sweet triumph of divinity taking hold of our spirit and soul!

Such 'suffering' of standing strong and staying true to God must be done with perseverance and humility, as we continue to draw closer to God, in reverence, abiding in the love of God and the resurrection power of the Blood of Christ. In essence, God has to be glorified, and the flesh and soul mortified. Even in the fire, we have choices. We can choose our level of abandonment, our level of mortification, and how much we seek to be purified. To reach the inner chambers of God's throne room, we must never hesitate in our mortification, but let God's power and fire refine and set us free from our inner turmoil and strife.

It is only when we discover the path of God's wonderful presence, will and truth that the power of the external world in terms of interest and its power of bondage is broken. We must turn to God so that God can, through divine unity, brings forth healing and deliverance. The essence and truth of the fire were on a deeper level explored in the teachings, for example by French Christians such as Molinos, Guyon and Fenelon during the 1600s.

The substance of the fire burning within a believer is summed up beautifully in the following two statements:

It is the fire of suffering which will bring forth the gold of godliness (Guyon)

And finally, none of us as believers will be purified except in the fire of inward pain. (Molinos)

Molinos described five steps toward the inward way. The first is enlightenment. In this stage, divine affection is kindled. Divine love for Him dries up those things which are but human.

There follows, secondly, an inward anointing. Something like a liquid Spirit flows into the believer's being, teaches him, strengthens him and allows him to receive a deeper understanding of the Lord and His way. With this comes a pleasure that seems heavenly.

The third stage is the growth of the inward man, the spiritual man. As the inward man begins to grow stronger than the outer man a clear foundation of pure love for the Lord arises.

Next comes illumination. Illumination is something from the Spirit of God to the human spirit which dwells within man.

At last, there is peace. Tranquillity. A victory over all fighting has come internally. Peace and joy are great. The believer seems to rest, as one abiding in Divine and loving arms.

The first stage is to do with Salvation, when the Holy Spirit convicts us of our need to accept Jesus as our Saviour (enlightenment), revealing that we are completely lost without God's direction. Love fills us, as our spirit is connected to God. The second and third stages are part of the baptism of the Holy Spirit. As we surrender to the Spirit, allowing our spirit and soul to be submerged under God's hand, we are guided in truth. The anointing comes through fellowship and obedience. In truth and freedom, which come by living according to the Spirit, we grow spiritually. The fourth and fifth stages are part of the process of the fire. The refining fire is the illumination of our 'inner demons', allowing us to mortify and then to be purified. This process draws us to God, which results in peace and tranquillity.

By drawing inwardly, our prayer life increases, for now, there is a divine union between our spirit and soul with God, allowing for words to become unnecessary. In the Holy of Holies, God in all His glory is present. As in the days of the tabernacle, no words are spoken, for God and man are united. External expressions, thoughts, or words are of no use, for God enters our spirit and soul, and there is then a divine inner communication. In divine unity and divine love, our soul and spirit flow like liquid fire into God's Spirit, allowing for internal prayer. When we draw inward towards the centre of God, no words are needed, for now, our spirit and God's spirit are completely joined, and God speaks into our spirit and soul. In internal prayer, there is a silence of words, thoughts, and desires. God is all. He is at the heart of your spirit, and we must allow God to move in our souls.

The fire is, in conclusion, the deeper cry of the spirit of man to be melted and united with God, who is Spirit. To reach such a state, we have to go through the continual fire of suffering and refinement, thus the reality of John 15, so that God can produce the gold of godliness within us. Daily God does indeed convict us of our sin, as His fire searches our hearts. Yet, just as we completely surrender to the Holy Spirit when we are baptised, so we must be willing to completely surrender to the fire that produces refinement and purity.

# Spontaneous word: There is a glorious flow of the Spirit

Indeed, by the Spirit, there is a glorious flow where the Spirit of God leads, where the fire burns and where His glory resides. There is a glorious flow of His might and power. And this glorious flow is in the light and beauty of essence divine, where the rod blossoms and where the cup of the Lord feeds the hungry heart. It is the flow of truth and the light. There is a glorious flow from the Throne and from the heart of Majesty, and all those who flow and all those who seek such flow shall flow in Him, and they shall indeed be set free to flow in His glory and majesty.

God never intended His people to be ordinary or commonplace. He intended that they should be on fire for Him, conscious of His divine power, realising the glory of the cross that foreshadows the crown. We cannot serve man and God. We cannot serve the kingdoms of the world and the Kingdom of Heaven. If we do, we bow before two altars. If we do so, we burn with God's fire and profane fire. This cannot be. It is time again that we return to the Covenant by committing our very lives again to the Lord, so that there is a cry in our heart, we will serve no other God and that He is our First Love and He is our Master and Lord! There is only the Covenant with one spiritual master that should be in place – and that is with God. And then we shall be on fire with God – yes, burning with passion and compassion!

There is a mighty flow of healing, and there is a mighty flow of His Spirit for all those who will heed and listen and come unto Him, for there is a mighty flow where the eagle flies and where the lion roams and where the sky meets the earth and where heaven extends an open hand. It is the flow of the Spirit, and in such flow is the fire of God that burns, burns and burns.

How the Lord yearns for our hearts to be set on fire for God by the Spirit of God. By such fire to burn for God. To burn for His Kingdom. To burn in love. To burn to save the lost. To burn to tell the world of Jesus. How the Lord cries for us to come into this open flow, and into the flow of majesty and power and glory. Come into the flow of His majesty and power and grace. For there is a flow like liquid gold, pouring, pouring, and pouring, but we need to come, we need to kneel, we need to drink, and we need to come with a hungry and a thirsty heart. It is the flow of the holy fire of God where the Spirit dwells and moves.

How we need to come with a spirit that is yearning and longing and hungry, giving up all, surrendering, humble and contrite. For then we shall burn for God in the fire of the Spirit. How we need to come to give all, to lay all down, to bare all, to have nothing left, for there is a flow in the Spirit that no man can stop, that no weapon can counter and that no power can even resist, for this is the mighty flow of the Spirit for those who believe and those who listen and to those who obey and to those who seek Him above all.

There is a mighty flow for those who come to the mountain, where the hand of the Almighty and the hand of man meet, where the wings of the angelic hosts meet the tassels of the prayer shawl, and where the hungry heart of mankind melts into the love divine. Glory, glory, glory, and let us sing hallelujah, for we cannot fully understand or see or comprehend this mighty flow and this mighty presence of Him who is divine and glorious, for there is a mighty flow of His grace and mercy unto those who come to the mountain to seek Him in the silence, embracing the thunder, and running not from the extended hand of love and mercy.

There is a mighty flow of the fire by the Spirit where the earth splits and the ground gives way and the mountain quakes, for this is a place where the ladder of Jacob is planted and where the Lord makes the earth His footstool. Seek Him not in the dust and seek Him not in the skies, for the Lord says seek Him where we may go and seek Him where we may wander, for wander we shall, but we need to seek as the yearning, and we need to seek as the longing and we need to seek beyond the veil and beyond the wall and beyond the mind. We need to seek beyond, there where the eagle nests and where the lion sleeps. We need to wander where the angelic hosts come to speak, where the cities crumble, where Babylon quakes, and where Jerusalem is established.

It is all about the cross. Come into the shadow of the Almighty, come into the embrace of truth and love, and then love will cast away doubt. For at the Cross, the skies opened and the way for the Spirit, thus the path for the fire, was opened. We need to let love bind up the broken heart and let love mend the way of the fallen and the shattered. There is a mending, a mending divine, a mending indeed of God's ways by the cross. For the love divine mends and it binds and it soothes. Come all who are wounded and bruised unto Him who was first wounded and bruised, and be set free in His glory and majesty forever and ever.

For the Lord says freedom! And He cries deliverance! Unto those who come into the flow of God, and unto His love and hope divine. Indeed, there is a mighty flow where the wings of divinity enfold over the shame and the guilt, and where the wings enfold, a covenant abides, and in the abiding let there be a resting and in the resting a deeper conviction of sparkling hope. Come and drink from the waters. Come and drink from the fountain. Be our life Lord, be our hope Lord, and may we rest under Your Wings – there where the flow flows and the

Spirit moves and the love divine sets free. For this is the place where we find the fire of God, always burning.

Hallelujah, praise the Lord, for who cannot but sing of His great love and mercy, which is so pure and perfect and gracious. Who cannot but sing of His beauty and majesty? Shall we not come and kneel, and give all? Shall we not come and kneel, and abide? Shall we not come and just give all? For the Holy Spirit flows and He wants to move in man in power and glory, but oh, why do we so resist cries the Spirit? Give up your heart, give up all, and let the glorious Spirit fill and consume until His Presence drips like oil from lips and eyes and soul reconciled unto God Almighty. For then we shall know the fire. We shall walk in it and taste it goodness. Come Holy Spirit, come oh Lord, and consume, for let this be our heart's desire, for Your Presence like manifested oil upon us, for Your Presence like a manifested breath within us. For Your Presence like manifested healing.

There is a flow, a mighty flow of healing and power! There is a mighty flow and there is healing, there is deliverance, but we need to come into the flow, we need to come into the stream, and indeed, we must rest, we must abide, we must behold, we must belong, and we must give all cries to the Lord. We must burn in the Spirit so that our very beings are set on fire for God!

Surrender hearts stubborn, and a soul resistant to His flow. Submit, and yearn and long for His majesty and grace. He is awesome, He is mighty, and he is the Lord Divine who broke the hand of Egypt and the might of Babylon. He brought Rome to its knees, and so again He will bring to the knee those who exalt and those who resist Him. Come to the mountain for the Lord. Rest, and come and drink and come and be fed!

Shall we stand in His breath; shall we partake of His execution of will and purpose? Shall we reside under the shadow of His wing? Let all creation shout Glory! Let all creation shout Hallelujah! The Lord is on the move, and His feet rest on mountains and on hill tops. His feet, dressed in sandals, disturb the strongholds just like the dust parts and the ground shakes. His feet bring the Good News, but this almighty God shall not stop moving and flowing. For the dust shall part, and the way shall part, for the Lord is coming in all His glory and majesty!

Who shall resist? Praise Him! Let us sing to His glory. He parts His arms and the creation sighs with longing. He opens His mouth, and creation lives. He moves, and Creation moves. He is the flow, and He is Almighty. Come to Me says the Lord, and let Me show you the higher way, the deeper way, the true way, where the eagle resides, where the lion sleeps, where the hungry is fed, and the poor is satisfied. A highway indeed, there is a highway, shall we walk in His way, and find His glorious mysteries unfolding unto those who are planted like trees by the Living Streams of life?

He is Jesus, He is Lord, and shall we not bow and heed and give our all? Praise Him, Praise Him! Let us come, let us come and submit, and find rest in His embrace and arms, and let us know He is Almighty and Glorious and full of hope and truth and life. Let not the fire be quenched, and let not the flame perish, for let it burn, let it burn, let it burn forever!

Imagine if pulpits were again filled with the true words of God, as spoken by the Spirit? Words of conviction, for this surely will drive men and women to repentance! Words of pure fire. Yet we are more concerned about the Self and our needs, instead of reaching and teaching the Kingdom of God that will save man from the fires of hell and the pit of damnation. We need to speak as God leads, for this will cut men's heart.

Let it burn. We must not resist or quench the fire.

# Look, the Lord knocks:
# Be warm or cold, just not
# lukewarm

We are living in the days of the Laodicea church – a church found in Revelation 3 to be neither hot nor cold, but just lukewarm. We know the Scripture well, but there are a couple of key points to be found in this Scripture, which are often not realised that we need to understand, comprehend and ponder.

We find the Scripture reads as follows: 14 "And to the angel of the church of the Laodiceans write, 'These things says the Amen, the Faithful and True Witness, the Beginning of the creation of God: 15 "I know your works, that you are neither cold nor hot. I could wish you were cold or hot. 16 So then, because you are lukewarm, and neither cold nor hot, I will vomit you out of My mouth. 17 Because you say, 'I am rich, have become wealthy, and have need of nothing'—and do not know that you are wretched, miserable, poor, blind, and naked— 18 I counsel you to buy from Me gold refined in the fire, that you may be rich; and white garments, that you may be clothed, that the shame of your nakedness may not be revealed; and anoint your eyes with eye salve, that you may see. 19 As many as I love, I rebuke and chasten. Therefore be zealous and repent. 20 Behold, I stand at the door and knock. If anyone hears My voice and opens the door, I will come in to him and dine with him, and he with Me. 21 To him who overcomes I will grant to sit with Me on My throne, as I also overcame and sat down with My Father on His throne. 22 "He who has an ear, let him hear what the Spirit says to the churches."'

Few can argue with the reality that we live in a time where churches are fixated on wealth accumulation, on riches, self-glorification, and we do not even know that we are wretched, miserable, poor, blind, and naked. This is of great concern, as the Lord is returning for a Bride without spot or wrinkle (clothed in white garments). And such clothing speaks about how we are supposed to be clothed with Christ for the Scripture says in "Galatians 3: 26 For you are all sons of God through faith in Christ Jesus. 27 For as many of you as were baptized into Christ have put on Christ. The Amplified Bible states it as follows: 27 For all of you who were baptized into Christ [into a spiritual union with the Christ, the Anointed] have clothed yourselves with Christ [that is, you have taken on His characteristics and values]."

The idea of being clothed also speaks of the concept, as brought forward by Paul when mentioning the armour of God in Ephesians 6. In Revelation 3, we also read: But you [still] have a few people in Sardis who have not soiled their clothes [that is, contaminated their character and personal integrity with sin]; and they will walk with Me [dressed] in white, because they are worthy (righteous). He who overcomes [the world through believing that Jesus is the Son of God] will accordingly be dressed in white clothing; and I will never blot out his name from the Book of Life, and I will confess and openly acknowledge his name before My Father and before His angels [saying that he is one of Mine].

Being clothed speaks of being found ready and not naked in the presence of the Lord. For it says in Revelation 16:15: "Behold, I am coming like a thief. Blessed is he who stays awake and who keeps his clothes [that is, stays spiritually ready for the Lord's return], so that he will not be naked—spiritually unprepared—and men will not see his shame."

We are reminded of the following in the "Book of Jude: 20 But you, beloved, build yourselves up on [the foundation of] your most holy faith [continually progress, rise like an edifice higher and higher], pray in the Holy Spirit, 21 and keep yourselves in the love of God, waiting anxiously and looking forward to the mercy of our Lord Jesus Christ [which will bring you] to eternal life. 22 And have mercy on some, who are doubting; 23 save others, snatching them out of the fire; and on some have mercy but with fear, loathing even the clothing spotted and polluted by their shameless immoral freedom."

We read about clothing being spotted and polluted by their shameless immoral freedom. This is after all the time we live in. A time of immorality and where what is natural to God is now unnatural to man. This is a time of excesses, liberties and decadence. Sadly, not only does the world indulge in such gratifications, but also many believers, and thus spoil their clothes to a point of being found naked in the presence of the Lord because of sin and iniquity.

In Revelation 3, the Lord was speaking spiritually, and how because of the fallen state of this church, the believers were spiritually impoverished and they were spiritually blind and naked (which speaks of a sense of shame and guilt because of the lust of the flesh and lust of the eyes - 1 John 2:16). After all, the word "naked" reminds us of the Garden where Adam and Eve were left naked because of their disobedience, listening to the devil, and so they found themselves naked in their guilt and naked in their guilt. Yet our nakedness on a spiritual level is truly covered by the Blood of Jesus when we come to Him to receive our acceptance, restoration, salvation, redemption and hope. We are clothed in Christ because of our obedience, faithfulness, love, faith and hope in Him.

This entire passage reminds us also of the words of Jesus when He spoke in Mark 4 to His disciples regarding the parable of the Sower: 10 But when He was alone, those around Him with the twelve asked Him about the parable. 11 And He said to them, "To you it has been given to know the mystery of the kingdom of God; but to those who are outside, all things come in parables, 12 so that 'Seeing they may see and not perceive, And hearing they may hear and not understand; Lest they should turn, And their sins be forgiven them.'"

You see, the church of the Laodiceans was encouraged to find their spiritual vision and sight in God, for it is written that the Lord counselled them to buy from [HIM] gold refined in the fire .... So that their eyes may be anointed "with eye salve, that you may see". Of course, when we read "refined in fire", we think of Malachi 3, where it is written: 2 But who can endure the day of His coming? And who can stand when He appears? For He is like a refiner's fire and like a launderer's soap [which removes impurities and uncleanness]. Note how soap removed stains, for in our Lord we find our righteousness, and we are clothed as such, but then we need to submit, yield and trust in Him. Our God is a consuming fire, and as Paul wrote in Galatians, He shall not be mocked.

Indeed, once we truly "see" the Kingdom of God, meaning we see beyond our carnality, our selfish nature, the natural, the bondages, the hurt and the pain, we then begin to understand and comprehend the Glory of the Kingdom. For once God restores our spiritual sight, so does our perception of the natural and supernatural changes, and so we begin to walk from glory to glory. The question of spiritual sight was also raised by Jesus when He said in John 3: "Most assuredly, I say to you, unless one is born again, he cannot see the kingdom of God." The Lord in His ministry did cause the blind to see, but truly His greatest desire is for us to "see" spiritually and to "behold" Him as our true salvation, hope and redemption. Once we lose sight of him, we become lost in the maze of worldly images and ideas that only seek to enslave.

Yes, God counselled the church to buy gold from Him to be rich, and to be clothed, and again, this speaks volumes of spiritual riches, spiritual treasures and seeking the Kingdom of God above all. This reminds of the Scripture that says in Colossians 2: For I want you to know what a great conflict I have for you and those in Laodicea, and for as many as have not seen my face in the flesh, 2 that their hearts may be encouraged, being knit together in love, and attaining to all riches of the full assurance of understanding, to the knowledge of the mystery of God, both of the Father and of Christ, 3 in whom are hidden all the treasures of wisdom and knowledge.

The greatest riches and treasure we should seek is God Himself, in whom rests all the glory, wisdom and knowledge. This is why it states that we must first seek the Kingdom and His Righteousness above all, for then the rest shall be added. After all, we must store up riches in heaven. For it says in Isaiah 55: "1 Ho! Everyone who thirsts, Come to the waters; and you who have no money, Come, buy and eat. Yes, come, buy wine and milk without money and without price. 2 Why do you spend money for what is not bread, and your wages for what does not satisfy? Listen carefully to Me, and eat what is good, And let your soul delight itself in abundance."

There is much more to be said on the matter, but the reality is that the church of the Laodiceans had drifted away from the Lord, from His ways, His holiness and Glory. They had become spiritually poor, blind and naked for they were seeking the things of the world and have lost their way. They were left spiritually naked, and no longer clothed by His royalty. After all, as Peter wrote, we are a holy priesthood when clothed by Him and when we stand in Covenant with our Lord. We are very much in similar times, where the world has blinded us to the truth, purity and holiness of God.

Now, let us discuss the matter of being lukewarm for there is great misunderstanding about this. Notice also how Isaiah 55 speaks about the question of thirst and water. Naturally, this reminds us of the teaching by Jesus in "John 7: 37 On the last day, that great day of the feast, Jesus stood and cried out, saying, "If anyone thirsts, let him come to Me and drink. 38 He who believes in Me, as the Scripture has said, out of his heart will flow rivers of living water." 39 But this He spoke concerning the Spirit, whom those believing in Him would receive; for the Holy Spirit was not yet given, because Jesus was not yet glorified."

With all of this to reflect upon, to understand the concept of being lukewarm, let us first consider the geographical location of the church of the Laodiceans. We need to understand that the town had to settle for lukewarm water which was being fed to them via an aqueduct, and the waters were definitely not as favourable as the hot springs at nearby Hierapolis or the cold, pure waters of Colossae. The archaeology shows Laodicea, therefore, had an aqueduct that probably carried water from hot mineral springs some five miles south, which would have become tepid before entering the city.

Generally, when we look at this Scripture, we think that Jesus was implying that "hot" is good and "cold" is bad. The traditional view has been that the Laodiceans were being criticised for their neutrality or lack of zeal (hence "lukewarm"). If we study the qualities of water, and the hot and cold water found in the nearby towns, we discover that both hot and cold water are useful, whereas lukewarm water is emetic.

You see, Jesus was not saying to the church to be hot and not cold in terms of their passion or zeal for Him; He was rather saying, "be useful, be fruitful and be productive for the Kingdom". You see, Jesus was saying be hot OR cold, it doesn't matter, because both are good, but DO NOT BE LUKEWARM. To be lukewarm also implies an uncommitted stance, and it speaks of compromise and polluting the pureness of the Lord and the Word with our ideals and self-glorification. It speaks of contamination (of our spiritual state).

Of such a state of being lukewarm Paul writes in "2 Timothy 3: But know this, that in the last days perilous times will come: 2 For men will be lovers of themselves, lovers of money, boasters, proud, blasphemers, disobedient to parents, unthankful, unholy, 3 unloving, unforgiving, slanderers, without self-control, brutal, despisers of good, 4 traitors, headstrong, haughty, lovers of pleasure rather than lovers of God, 5 having a form of godliness but denying its power. And from such people turn away! 6 For of this sort are those who creep into households and make captives of gullible women loaded down with sins, led away by various lusts, 7 always learning and never able to come to the knowledge of the truth."

We need to understand that while hot or cold water is useful and has good qualities, lukewarm water has no usage and is a breeding ground for germs. And considering Jesus taught about the living waters, it makes us realise that as long as we are not completely committed to the Lord and to His Way and Truth, then we begin to pollute the waters. Then how can the Holy Spirit - He who leads us in all truth, power, wisdom, might, knowledge and counsel – lead us in the pure way of the Lord? For then surely we are blind, for remember, we "SEE" the Kingdom of God once we are reborn in the Spirit (the living waters).

Therefore, let us be HOT OR COLD, implying being useful for the Kingdom, but let us not be lukewarm. This reminds us of John 15: "I am the true vine, and My Father is the vinedresser. 2 Every branch in Me that does not bear fruit He takes away; and every branch that bears fruit He prunes, that it may bear more fruit. 3 You are already clean because of the word which I have spoken to you. 4 Abide in Me, and I in you. As the branch cannot bear fruit of itself, unless it abides in the vine, neither can you, unless you abide in Me. 5 "I am the vine, you are the branches. He who abides in Me, and I in him, bears much fruit; for without Me you can do nothing. 6 If anyone does not abide in Me, he is cast out as a branch and is withered; and they gather them and throw them into the fire, and they are burned.

Now, as a last and most important point, we come to the Scripture: "20 Behold, I stand at the door and knock. If anyone hears My voice and opens the door, I will come in to him and dine with him, and he with Me." We have often contextualised this Scripture to apply it to those who must still come to the Lord and be saved. However, in the context of the Scripture, Jesus was standing at the door of the church of the Laodiceans and knocking. Now, if someone is knocking, it means they are on the outside. Therefore, Jesus was not even present in the church, because He was still outside, knocking to be allowed in. And why was He outside? Because the church had drifted away from Him and had sought fame and riches, and so they have been lukewarm. Therefore, Jesus was no longer even in their midst anymore.

Let me take you back to Genesis 3 at the fall of mankind. Remember, Adam and Eve once walked in the Garden with the Lord (He was in their midst). Then we read, "8 And they heard the sound of the Lord God walking in the garden in the cool [afternoon breeze] of the day, so the man and his wife hid and kept themselves hidden from the presence of the Lord God among the trees of the garden." Adam and Eve had created a distance between themselves and God because of sin and their disobedience. This "distance" was restored by the Blood of Jesus, but still, we push God away because of sins, iniquity, immorality and apostasy that lead us to shame and trying to cover ourselves with "leaves" (speaking of worldly attempts at self-justification and righteousness).

It also says in "Revelation 22:14 Blessed (happy, prosperous, to be admired) are those who wash their robes [in the blood of Christ by believing and trusting in Him—the righteous who do His commandments], so that they may have the right to the tree of life, and may enter by the gates into the city. 15 Outside are the dogs [the godless, the impure, those of low moral character] and the sorcerers [with their intoxicating drugs, and magic arts], and the immoral persons [the perverted, the molesters, and the adulterers], and the murderers, and the idolaters, and everyone who loves and practices lying (deception, cheating). Indeed, there is the distance created between God and ourselves when we walk a road of impurity, immorality and debauchery (also see the work of the flesh in Galatians 5)."

We need to understand that this is the state of our church these days as well. God has been pushed out of the door in our churches because we have sought to follow our own agendas, running after religion, fame, fortune, status, wealth, and self-glory as we build our own kingdoms that will eventually stumble and fall. We have exchanged His glory for our own, His Truth for our own brand of moral relativism, and we have made ourselves god to suit our own needs. And so we stand spiritually naked, wretched and poor, yet we do not even know it. We have allowed the fire of the Spirit to die and to e quenched!

And yes, we read of how the Lord is calling and how we must hear Him. It says in "John 10: 1 I assure you and most solemnly say to you, he who does not enter by the door into the sheepfold, but climbs up from some other place [on the stone wall], that one is a thief and a robber. 2 But he who enters by the door is the shepherd of the sheep [the protector and provider]. 3 The doorkeeper opens [the gate] for this man, and the sheep hear his voice and pay attention to it. And [knowing that they listen] he calls his own sheep by name and leads them out [to pasture]. 4 When he has brought all his own sheep outside, he walks on ahead of them, and the sheep follow him because they know his voice and recognize his call. 5 They will never follow a stranger, but will run away from him, because they do not know the voice of strangers." 6 Jesus used this figure of speech with them, but they did not understand what He was talking about."

Can you hear it? The Lord is still knocking on the door of the church, and He is still saying that if we allow Him in, He will dine with us. He is the DOOR, He is the Way, and we choose to ignore the knock at our own peril. He cries out to us to allow Him in, but sadly, so many in the churches do not even know Him and do not recognise His voice. They are like Samuel of 1 Samuel 4, who could not recognise the Lord's calling. He wants to be our Lord, King and Master again, yet so often we have pushed Him away.

To dine with us speaks of friendship, it speaks of companionship, and it speaks of communion; therefore, COVENANT. What is the Lord, therefore, saying? I AM KNOCKING, SO ALLOW ME IN -

ALLOW ME INTO YOUR LIFE FOR I AM THE WAY, TRUTH AND LIFE – ALLOW ME IN SO THAT YOU and I MAY BE IN COVENANT.

We have pushed the Lord out of the door, and we cannot hear Him knocking because the screams of our idolatry, apostasy and reckless pursuit of the glory of the world have deafened us to His knocking and to His voice. We have become blinded to His presence, blinded to His glory and blinded to His Truth, for we have allowed the veil of religion, tradition and legalisms to blind us. We have become so preoccupied with our own needs, wants and desires that we have lost sight of the Lord, who is knocking and crying out to His flock. Indeed, it also reminds us of Ezekiel 10 where the Glory of the Lord left the temple because of the iniquity and idolatry of the people. Truly, He is knocking, yet we drown Him out with our brand of worship, emotionalism and spirituality.

He is crying out for a pure and holy Bride, clothed with Him, who seeks Him above all else, and who seeks not after the gold and silver of the world. A church that is on fire for God! Yes, the Lord is still knocking. Will we answer? For then, as we seek Him, we shall be in Covenant and be hot or cold, but not lukewarm, and the living waters shall flow from us, and we shall be the light and the salt of a broken word. He is knocking. Are we blind or deaf, or shall we hear, shall we see, and shall we open the door?

# The fire of our calling

Some, however few, people may wonder why I keep on writing. Some may think I do so for profit. Others may think I do so for recognition or some kind of status. It has actually nothing to do with money or supposed fame. It has to do with the fire of God.

We read in Jeremiah 20 of how the prophet, at the same time while he is lamenting his calling, says the following "7 O Lord, You induced me, and I was persuaded; You are stronger than I, and have prevailed. I am in derision daily; everyone mocks me. 8 For when I spoke, I cried out; I shouted, "Violence and plunder!" Because the word of the Lord was made to me a reproach and a derision daily. 9 Then I said, "I will not make mention of Him, nor speak anymore in His name." But His word was in my heart like a burning fire shut up in my bones; I was weary of holding it back, And I could not."No matter what Jeremiah was going though, he could NOT keep silent because the Word of God burned in his heart and burned in his bones. After all, our Lord is an all-consuming fire. Jeremiah 23:29 says: "Is not my word like fire," declares the LORD, "and like a hammer that breaks a rock in pieces?" God's Word is like fire. And God wants His Word to burn like fire in us!

Our calling is also the fire that burns in our spirit, in our bones and heart. Whenever we truly connect with our calling/mandate, then we shall connect with that fire. The fire of God empowers and equips us to fulfil our calling. It is the Holy Spirit that burns deep within us to bring forth the purified gold of the calling, so that we may fulfil what

God has ordained us to complete. The closer we move to the fire, the greater the conviction, the passion, the yearning and the desire to run with one's calling. For everyone has a calling from God, and that calling ultimately burns in our bones like fire. It is a fire you cannot escape, no matter how hard you try. It is unyielding, unflinching and unwavering in design and purpose. Once we submit to the calling, we allow the fire to burn in us until all that we can do is to allow the fire to complete its fiery purpose!

Paul endured much suffering, yet he ran the race and kept the faith. His mandate was to deliver the Good News to the Gentiles. It was the fire that burned in his heart and bones. It is a fire that cannot be ignored. It is a fire that one cannot turn away from. The closer one draws to God in fellowship and intimacy, the deeper one dwells in the fire, and the stronger the fire burns. And the stronger the fire burns, the stronger the need and the want to do as the Lord commands and ordains. If one is really connected with God, you are connected with the fire of your calling. As God is an all-consuming fire, we must be consumed by our calling and mandate.

To put what Jeremiah said in context, remember he was frequently attacked and rejected for what he said. When faithfully obeying God, he was accused of being manipulative and speaking without authority. In Jeremiah 15 we read of his distress, "10 Alas, my mother, that you gave me birth, a man with whom the whole land strives and contends! I have neither lent nor borrowed, yet everyone curses me. 11 The Lord said, "Surely I will deliver you for a good purpose; surely I will make your enemies plead with you in times of disaster and times of distress." We can imagine how much yielding to the fire must have frustrated him. He knew he was obeying the Lord, yet people consistently attacked him. Discouraged, Jeremiah tried to escape this difficult mission. He thought of trying to forget about God, saying, "I will not remember Him." And he resolved not to "speak any more in His name."

Yet try as he would, Jeremiah found it impossible to ignore the words God had given him, for it felt "like a burning fire shut up in my bones; and I am weary of holding it in, and I cannot endure it." He knew God had called him. The Lord's presence was so real, the burden of His message was so strong, that Jeremiah could not resist. He had to continue serving God, regardless of the consequences. Jeremiah discovered that obeying God does not guarantee popularity or freedom from difficulties. But it does guarantee that He will be pleased, and we will experience His blessings, both in this life and the life to come.

In Jeremiah 19, God, for example, gave his prophet a word to speak to Israel. Then he sent him into the temple court to prophesy. Jeremiah spoke these words: "Thus saith the Lord of hosts, the God of Israel; Behold, I will bring upon this city and upon all her towns all the evil that I have pronounced against it, because they have hardened their necks, that they might not hear my words" (Jeremiah 19:15). Pashur was chief governor of the temple at the time. And he was incensed by Jeremiah's words. Immediately, he flew into a rage and struck the prophet. Then he called forth his hirelings to lock up Jeremiah in stocks. He was to be placed at the city gate, where he would be humiliated for all to see. The stock was an instrument of torture. And Jeremiah would be in constant pain for a full twenty-four hours. First, his head was locked into position. Then his body was contorted, with his arms locked crosswise. He would have to remain in that torturous position for a night and a day.

What a horrifying scene. Remember, Jeremiah was an anointed prophet of the Lord. He'd known from his youth that he was called to speak God's Word to his chosen people. But now Jeremiah was bound up and tortured for doing just that. Yet, in spite of his suffering, Jeremiah never doubted his calling. He knew the Word he'd been given from God. And it had been that way from the very beginning of his ministry. The Lord himself had testified of his relationship with Jeremiah.

In Jeremiah 1 we read, "4 The word of the Lord came to me, saying, 5 "Before I formed you in the womb I knew you, before you were born I set you apart; I appointed you as a prophet to the nations." 6 "Alas, Sovereign Lord," I said, "I do not know how to speak; I am too young." 7 But the Lord said to me, "Do not say, 'I am too young.' You must go to everyone I send you to and say whatever I command you. 8 Do not be afraid of them, for I am with you and will rescue you," declares the Lord. 9 Then the Lord reached out his hand and touched my mouth and said to me, "I have put my words in your mouth. 10 See, today I appoint you over nations and kingdoms to uproot and tear down, to destroy and overthrow, to build and to plant."

What an incredible moment in Jeremiah's life. How wonderful to know that God has put his hand on you, revealed to you His thoughts, and anointed you to speak for Him. Here was why Jeremiah never doubted the words God gave him. In the same chapter, we read, "17 Get yourself ready! Stand up and say to them whatever I command you. Do not be terrified by them, or I will terrify you before them. 18 Today I have made you a fortified city, an iron pillar and a bronze wall to stand against the whole land—against the kings of Judah, its officials, its priests and the people of the land. 19 They will fight against you but will not overcome you, for I am with you and will rescue you," declares the Lord."

God reminded Jeremiah it was God's word He was speaking and he was acting on behalf of God. If he lost sight of this reality, he would flame out. Whenever we look at ourselves and take our eyes away from God, we'll end up bitter and worn out, and we might even quit. God reminded Jeremiah that it doesn't matter what hardships he faced or how badly people treated or abused him, that they will never prevail. Indeed, God had put brass walls and mighty pillars surrounding the prophet. Similarly, we must keep our eyes upon God. We must be true to the fire of our calling. We must trust in God, and we must remain obedient. For God is with us and He will empower and strengthen us to fulfil such a calling.

This message is for everyone who, like Jeremiah, has been called from before creation to serve Christ. The apostle Paul says of God, "Who hath saved us, and called us with a holy calling, not according to our works, but according to his own purpose and grace, which was given us in Christ Jesus before the world began" (2 Timothy 1:9). Simply put, every person who is "in Christ" is called by the Lord. And we all have a mandate to hear God's voice, to proclaim his Word, to never fear man, and to trust the Lord in the face of every conceivable trial. We are all called to fulfil the Great Commission, but we also have different talents and gifts (including spiritual). As we yield to God, we shall know our calling and task to His Glory, and with such a calling comes the fire. The more we yield to His will, the more the fire rages.

It reminds of Amos 3:8 where we read, "The Lord God has spoken! Who can but prophesy?" Yes, when we truly submit to His will, who can but not fulfil their calling and mandate to His honour? For it is the fire that we cannot deny or ignore. For God's flame burns bright when we simply allow ourselves to be the living sacrifices on the altar.

Scripture shows that Paul was tested as few ministers ever have been. Satan tried to kill him time after time. The so-called religious crowd rejected and ridiculed him. At times, even those who supported him left him abused and forsaken. But Paul was never confounded before men. He was never dismayed or put to shame before the world. And Paul never did burn out. On every occasion, he had an anointed word to speak from God, just when it was needed. The fact is, Paul simply wouldn't be shaken. He never did lose his trust in the Lord. Instead, he testified, "12 For this reason I also suffer these things; nevertheless I am not ashamed, for I know whom I have believed and am persuaded that He is able to keep what I have committed to Him until that Day." (2 Timothy 1).

We like Paul and Jeremiah can keep on burning for God when we abide in God, and thus abide in the Spirit. And by the Spirit is the fire, and in the fire, we shall find our calling and mandate. And whatever God has called us to accomplish for His Kingdom, know that no man or devil can stand against it until God's purpose has been completed. Such is the nature of God's Word, His power and the raging fire of the Spirit. Jeremiah and Paul ran their race, and by God's grace and love, we can run our race and hold onto the faith. We need to seek God and humbly submit where He leads us so that we may stay true and faithful to the fire of our calling.

# Prophetic word: Fiery light on the tomb

I see a tombstone being rolled away ... it is large, almost round like a wheel. No man can move this tombstone. No man can remove it. I see the tombstone moving from right to left, and as it moves, light shines into the tomb, for God is moving it by His power. God can move what cannot be moved, for He is God. Praise the Lord!

Glory to God! There is a light shining in the tomb. A bright light - a beautiful light. It shines from heaven. It is not a pale light. It is fiery, as fire burns in the light. It is a beautiful shining light, and it is warm, it is alive, and it is beautiful. It shines and shines so bright from heaven, and the Lord is speaking into my spirit that this is the same pillar of fiery light that led the Israelites in the wilderness. Yes, this is the same light shining upon the tomb.

I hear a powerful voice calling aloud: "Arise!" And with that command, I understand the Lord is speaking to what is dead and buried. But a light is shining for He is the light. "I am the Resurrection," says the Lord. I am the Light of Glory. I am Life. I am Hope.

"Arise!" And there is a trembling of the ground. There is a trembling of the earth. There is a spiritual trembling as the Lord speaks. There is a quaking and there is a quickening.

A quickening, I ask? Yes, it burns into my spirit. A quickening of the Lord's end-time movement. A quickening of His will and purpose within His people. A quickening of His power and glory in His children. It is quickened by the light and fire and by the life of His very being and will and word and Spirit. A quickening of what is dead to be resurrected.

And this I hear again: "A quickening of life!"

And I look at the tomb and at the fiery light, and I seek in my spirit from the Lord what is coming to life. "All that is dead and buried," says the Lord. And the Lord places in my spirit that in people are promises, plans and purposes that have become dead and buried. Callings have become dead and buried. Hopes and dreams have become buried. Faith has become buried. Hope has become buried. Love has become buried. For the world I see has weighed heavily upon so many like a tombstone rolled to cover the light.

Oh Lord, we praise you! For there is a singing in my soul! For God is alive and He is life. Come to Him, this I hear. Turn to Him and pursue Him and watch, yes watch, and hear, as the tombstone is rolled away and hear His voice and see, yes see, how what is buried and dead becomes alive. For in God is hope. In God is life. In God is the Word and the Promise.

Yes, the tombstone has been rolled away, and the Lord speaks to His children that He is quickening, for His power is moving, His glory rolls forth, and He will awaken and bring to life those who slumber, those who have become lost and those who have lost their faith and hope. Yes, there is fire, and by the fire there is life, there is hope, and there is a divine and fiery quickening by the Spirit.

"Arise!" says the Lord. Praise the Lord! He is the Resurrection and the Life. And look – the fiery light shines upon that which is dusted and forgotten. No more I hear the Lord say. NO MORE! For the Lord remembers. The Lord knows.

For this is the day and hour and time of the Lord. Lord, You call forth a people out of darkness, out of the decay and the dust to arise in Your light and to live in Your glory! A people arising in Your holy and majestic fire. Yes Lord, You speak to everyone who feels lost, who feels afraid, who is in darkness, who feels low in the spirit, who feels low in the soul, for You speak life and You speak hope! Yes Lord, in You there is life for You are the Life.

"For the tomb has been rolled away," says the Lord.

Jesus lives! He is the hope of our glory. Trust Him. Seek Him. Glory to God! The light shines brightly. The earth trembles. What has been forgotten shall no longer be forgotten. What has been hidden shall be brought into the light. What has been dead comes to life. God lives and God is true! Arise from your slumber for He speaks. We must open our eyes and ears and see and feel and hear Him. He is coming! He is coming! His light shines, and His glory shines, and He is coming to shake the earth.

Glory to our Lord! He brings us forth into a fiery light of redemption and hope. Let the light shine and let the fire burn.

# Shekinah fire

This is indeed for the true disciples to arise. Those who are bold and mighty in the Lord, those who are baptised and led by the Spirit. Disciples burning with Shekinah fire, and who walk in the truth of Acts 5 (verse 29), that one ought to obey God rather than men. Indeed, these are disciples who speak not like the scribes, but in the authority of God. They speak by God's wisdom, knowledge and understanding and foolishness is not found on their lips. Glory to God, they shall fight for the soul of the church, glorifying and praising Jesus, for they shall have no other king but Jesus! They seek only the will of God on earth as in heaven.

Jan Hus, the Reformer, once said: "Therefore faithful Christian, seek the truth, listen to the truth, learn the truth, love the truth, speak the truth, adhere to truth and defend truth to the death. For the truth will set you free from sin, the devil and the destruction of the soul, and ultimately from eternal death which is eternal separation from God's grace and the joy of salvation." Indeed, we can stand for the truth and defend it when God's fire of conviction burns within us! A fire that will not yield to the ways of the fallen world of the seductions of the devil.

So what is this Shekinah Glory that manifests also as Shekinah fire? We need to understand it is the visible manifestation of God on earth, whose presence is portrayed through a natural occurrence. The word Shekinah is a Hebrew name meaning "dwelling" or "one who dwells." Shekinah Glory means "He caused to dwell," referring to the divine presence of God. The word Shekinah is not in the Bible, but the description is.

In the classical Hebrew and Aramaic manuscripts of the Old and New Testaments, the word Shekinah is actually not found. It was first introduced by Jewish rabbis through targums and literature in the period between the completion of the Old Testament and the onset of the New Testament. The etymology of "Shekinah" is from the Hebrew word shākan, which means "to reside or permanently stay." It was, therefore, used to signify that it was a divine visitation of the presence or dwelling of the Lord God on this earth.

Some say the Shekinah was first evident when the Israelites set out from Succoth in their escape from Egypt. There the Lord appeared in a cloudy pillar in the day and a fiery pillar by night: "After leaving Succoth they camped at Etham on the edge of the desert. By day the LORD went ahead of them in a pillar of cloud to guide them on their way and by night in a pillar of fire to give them light, so that they could travel by day or night. Neither the pillar of cloud by day nor the pillar of fire by night left its place in front of the people" (Exodus 13:20–22). There is also some that say that when Moses encountered the burning bush, we find the first real manifestation of God after the flood. Thus, the first and real encounter with Shekinah fire! And it had to be God burning (dwelling) in the bush at the time, for He said to Moses to take off his shoes and proclaimed Himself I AM.

The visible manifestation of God's presence was seen not only by the Israelites but also by the Egyptians in Exodus 14: "24 Now it came to pass, in the morning watch, that the Lord looked down upon the army of the Egyptians through the pillar of fire and cloud, and He troubled the army of the Egyptians. 25 And He took off their chariot wheels, so that they drove them with difficulty; and the Egyptians said, "Let us flee from the face of Israel, for the Lord fights for them against the Egyptians." Just the presence of God's Shekinah glory was enough to convince His enemies that He was not someone to be resisted! Glory to God.

The rabbis used the term Shekinah to describe the following to the Jewish people:

•The presence of God among His people (Exodus 19:16-18; Exodus 40:34-38; I Kings 6:13)

•The glory of God dwelling in the Temple (2 Chronicles 7:1)

• How God dwells in the mountain (Psalm 68.16-18; Joel 3:17)

The divine presence of God, thus His very Shekinah Glory/Fire, on earth was for example in the Bible depicted through the following:

• As a cloud (Exodus 24:16-18; Exodus 33:9; 1 Kings 8:10-13)

• As a pillar of smoke and fire (Exodus 13:21-22)

• As fire and a burning bush (Zechariah 2:5; Exodus 3:2)

Moses certainly knew about the Shekinah Glory. Except for the burning bush experience, we read in "Exodus 34:29 Now it was so, when Moses came down from Mount Sinai (and the two tablets of the Testimony were in Moses' hand when he came down from the mountain), that Moses did not know that the skin of his face shone while he talked with Him." Moses was indeed on fire for God! Moses was experiencing the visible presence of God long before the coming of Jesus or the outpouring of the Holy Spirit! It reminds of "2 Corinthians 4:6 For it is the God who commanded light to shine out of darkness, who has shone in our hearts to give the light of the knowledge of the glory of God in the face of Jesus Christ."

Also consider when Moses pitched his tent outside of the Israelite camp in the wilderness to convene with God, how the latter spoke to Moses face to face through a cloud as though speaking to a friend (Exodus 33:11). However, when Moses asked to see God's face, He denied Moses' request, stating, "You cannot see my face, for no one may see me and live" (Exodus 33:20). The glory of God was too great for human eyes to gaze upon and survive. Instead, God allowed Moses to stand in a cleft in a rock and see God's back after He had passed by

(Exodus 33:21-23). For this reason, God appeared like a fire (Shekinah fire) in the bush as well. Moses, therefore, had numerous encounters with the Shekinah glory!

Elijah also had an encounter with God's manifested presence in 1 Kings 19 where we read, "11 Then He said, "Go out, and stand on the mountain before the Lord." And behold, the Lord passed by, and a great and strong wind tore into the mountains and broke the rocks in pieces before the Lord, but the Lord was not in the wind; and after the wind an earthquake, but the Lord was not in the earthquake; 12 and after the earthquake a fire, but the Lord was not in the fire; and after the fire a still small voice. 13 So it was, when Elijah heard it, that he wrapped his face in his mantle and went out and stood in the entrance of the cave. Suddenly a voice came to him, and said, "What are you doing here, Elijah?" Indeed, Elijah did not experience the Shekinah fire as experienced by Moses at the burning bush, but the Shekinah glory was very much evident on the mountain. Such presence bolstered Elijah to go forth and appoint Elisha as his successor.

In the New Testament, Jesus is the manifestation of Shekinah Glory. Jesus' ministry is the ultimate encounter of Shekinah Glory that God has ever had with man on earth. He was after all God who came in the flesh so that we may behold God, yet not in His absolute fullness of being pure spirit. Colossians 2:9-10 says, "For in Christ all the fullness of the Deity lives in bodily form, and in Christ you have been brought to fullness. He is the head over every power and authority." In Christ, we see the visible manifestation of God Himself in the second person of the Trinity. Although His glory was also veiled, Jesus is nonetheless the presence of God on earth. Just as the divine Presence dwelled in a relatively plain tent called the "tabernacle" before the Temple in Jerusalem was built, so did the Presence dwell in the human man who was Jesus. "He had no beauty or majesty to attract us to him, nothing in his appearance that we should desire him" (Isaiah 53:2). But when we get to heaven, we will see both the Son and the

Father in all their glory, and the Shekinah will no longer be veiled (1 John 3:2).

Remember, Jesus was made to be both God and man in one person, in order to act as our High Priest, so that He could be the embodiment of the redemption of our sins. Hebrews 2:17 says, "Therefore, in all things He had to be made like His brethren, that He might be a merciful and faithful High Priest in things pertaining to God, to make propitiation for the sins of the people." The separation of man from God was redeemed when Jesus paid the bond price for our sins with His blood on the Cross of Calvary. Upon His death, the veil separating the holiest of Holies in the Temple was torn, therefore, we are able to abide eternally in God's presence through a new covenant, with the Holy Spirit residing in us.

In the New Testament, Peter, John, and James also witnessed the Shekinah Glory of God during the Transfiguration of Jesus. This is an event where Jesus is transfigured and becomes radiant in glory upon a mountain. The Synoptic Gospels (Matthew 17:1–8, Mark 9:2–8, Luke 9:28–36) describe it, and the 2 Peter also refers to it (2 Peter 1:16–18). The account in Luke reads as follows: "28 Now it came to pass, about eight days after these sayings, that He took Peter, John, and James and went up on the mountain to pray. 29 As He prayed, the appearance of His face was altered, and His robe became white and glistening. 30 And behold, two men talked with Him, who were Moses and Elijah, 31 who appeared in glory and spoke of His decease which He was about to accomplish at Jerusalem. 32 But Peter and those with him were heavy with sleep; and when they were fully awake, they saw His glory and the two men who stood with Him. 33 Then it happened, as they were parting from Him, that Peter said to Jesus, "Master, it is good for us to be here; and let us make three tabernacles: one for You, one for Moses, and one for Elijah"—not knowing what he said. 34 While he was saying this, a cloud came and overshadowed them; and they were fearful as they entered the cloud."

The disciples experienced the 'cloud', thus the Shekinah Glory, just as the Israelites experienced God as a pillar of fire and smoke (also translated as a cloud) in the wilderness. Remember, this was even before the crucifixion, resurrection and ascension of Jesus. It was the same presence that we read about in Exodus 40 upon the tabernacle being set up by Moses: "34 Then the cloud covered the tabernacle of meeting, and the glory of the Lord filled the tabernacle. 35 And Moses was not able to enter the tabernacle of meeting, because the cloud rested above it, and the glory of the Lord filled the tabernacle. 36 Whenever the cloud was taken up from above the tabernacle, the children of Israel would go onward in all their journeys. 37 But if the cloud was not taken up, then they did not journey till the day that it was taken up. 38 For the cloud of the Lord was above the tabernacle by day, and fire was over it by night, in the sight of all the house of Israel, throughout all their journeys."

On the mount, the Lord gave His disciples a glimpse of His glory without the flesh. The vision of John, as recorded in the Book of Revelation, also beautifully described the radiant Jesus beyond the flesh. We read in Revelation 1, "12 I turned around to see the voice that was speaking to me. And when I turned I saw seven golden lampstands, 13 and among the lampstands was someone like a son of man, dressed in a robe reaching down to his feet and with a golden sash around his chest. 14 The hair on his head was white like wool, as white as snow, and his eyes were like blazing fire. 15 His feet were like bronze glowing in a furnace, and his voice was like the sound of rushing waters. 16 In his right hand he held seven stars, and coming out of his mouth was a sharp, double-edged sword. His face was like the sun shining in all its brilliance."

All of these encounters, except for John's visions, speak of a time before the outpouring of the Holy Spirit. On the Day of Pentecost, tongues of fire rested upon the disciples. This was the visible presence of God's glory by fire dwelling and resting with the believer of spirit, soul and body! This was the fulfilment of what John the Baptist said in "Matthew 3: 11 I baptize you with water for repentance. But after me comes one who is more powerful than I, whose sandals I am not worthy to carry. He will baptize you with the Holy Spirit and fire." The most incredible news is that by the infilling of the Holy Spirit, we as disciples of God carry the manifested presence of God within us! And for that reason, we can walk in the Shekinah fire of God by abiding in the Shekinah Glory. We do so by simply abiding in God, for then God will abide, thus dwell, in us (John 15).

Psalm 91 says, "He who dwells in the secret place of the Most High shall abide under the shadow of the Almighty." That "shadow" is indeed the cloud that manifested on the Transfiguration of Jesus. As we abide in Christ by the Spirit of God, we are walking in His glory daily. This is why we need to dwell in His presence and be so aware of it. We are now the vessels in which God resides by the Spirit, just as He was so present in the Holy of Holies in the tabernacle. 2 Corinthians 3:18 says, "But we all, with unveiled face, beholding as in a mirror the glory of the Lord, are being transformed into the same image from glory to glory, just as by the Spirit of the Lord." As we mature in Christ by dying to the self and as we yield and submit to the Holy Spirit, we shall indeed taste His goodness, know His power and manifest Shekinah fire! For all disciples, this is now a reality because of the Blood of the Lamb, because of the resurrection and the ascension, and because of Pentecost.

The manifestation of the Shekinah Glory and Fire is now not something merely external or pertaining to a few. For all believers reborn by the Spirit, this becomes a reality, for we are called to walk in God's glory, by His anointing of the Spirit, and empowered by the Blood and the Word. We are called to dwell in the Shekinah fire, encased and encapsulated, as we yield and submit to the Spirit of God, embracing God's presence and God's holy way. And there is great power in God's presence; therefore we must burn for God, so that God may burn in us to His glory!

# Seek the fire

Believers of the Lord, we must seek the fire! We must yearn for it! We must desire the presence of God. How hungry are you to dwell with God, to move in His glory? The fire of God is a fire of love, purity and power. We need His fire every day of our lives. We need it to overcome, to endure, to stand strong and to prosper in spirit, soul and body to the glory of God.

We need to remember that there is a fire, a fire of love that also burns for us. Did you know that God's heart burns with a blazing love for you? This is the reality of John 3:16, of the cross and the empty tomb! Everything God did from the beginning of time to the end of all things as we know it is for His creation to be reconciled unto Him. That is an awesome love! It is love that never changes, for God is constant, consistent and unfailing. A love that remains as so clearly spelt out in Romans 8. A love that is waiting to turn your life upside down. Ask God for His fire. Ask Him for this blaze of His love. Make it the most important prayer of your life: "Father, give me Your blazing fire of love. Let me be filled with that fire. Let me be on fire with you by the Spirit of God. Yes, Lord, send the fire to burn in me!"

Yet, we need to be hungry for such a fire. We need to hunger and yearn to receive this fire in our heart, the burning love of God, His burning presence, and His burning holy touch so that we shall be ignited by love to love more and to walk in holiness. By such fire, we will be changed to reach the world. This fire is stronger than death. This fire is more beautiful than life itself. This fire is more intense than anything that exists. Ask God for His fire to burn by the Spirit, for it is the baptism by the Spirit. Such fire comes from complete yielding and submission unto God.

Without the fire of God you live without true life, without passion. Without the fire of God, you have religion, human wisdom derived from the Bible and insights that appear to be godly but which do not result in the power of God. It is empty. It sounds nice, but it doesn't change lives. It doesn't heal the sick. It doesn't set the possessed free. It doesn't help the suffering. We need the fire to be changed and to change lives! It is the fire of Pentecost that birthed the Church! Yes, the fire of God changed Jerusalem into a place of fire on the day of Pentecost, when the Holy Spirit was poured out. How the Pentecost fire has been setting hearts aflame for God for hundreds of years! We need the presence of God! How we need the fire of God to burn intensely. The fire of God still lights up the hearts of people worldwide, and it changes them more than anything else.

Reality is that the blazing fire of God's love captures your heart and sets you on fire for the salvation of other people. For the fire that burns in God's heart should burn in us. How we need to be so on fire with love that consumes what is evil, love that moves like a whirlwind of compassion and commitment. Fire also cleanses. It purifies, for it burns away your self-fabricated image. Fire humbles you. Fire strips away the ragged garments, consumes the dirt and leaves you cleansed and free, so Jesus can clothe you with His humble garments. Fire is what we need. Ask for the fire of God.

With words alone, you will never reach the people who are lost. You can caress the carnal mind and intellectual, religious, hypocrisy of the sinful man, but that will not help anyone. We need the power of God. We need His Presence. We need His fire that shatters strongholds and sets the captives free!

Think about the parable of the virgins who had their beautifully polished Christian oil lamps with them, but only a few of them also had the oil that could make the FIRE burn. Scriptures say that at that time the kingdom of heaven will be like ten virgins who took their lamps and went out to meet the Bridegroom. Five of them were foolish and five were wise. The foolish ones took their lamps but did not take any oil with them. The wise, however, took oil in jars along with their lamps." (Matthew 25:1-4). Some were ready, on fire, and some had grown cold. Is your oil lamp empty? Or are you on fire for God? Ask for the oil so your fire can burn. Seek the Lord, yearn for Him, for only you can fellowship with Him! How the Lord desires true intimacy.

How easily do we not quench the fire because of our carnality, because we are so busy and we are so preoccupied with our lives and problems? Yet when we lay it all down, deny ourselves and carry the cross, we shall learn true yielding and submitting unto God. For then, the fire shall come, the fire shall burn, for the fire destroys our pride and ego. For God is in the fire of humility, in the gentleness and kindness. For God is a loving God. His love is fire. God is pure fire, real fire. How we need to be changed by that fire! Yes, Lord, burn through our pride and defences with your consuming fire. Make us real, Lord. Make us blaze with Your fire, Lord. Full us Lord in the eternal fire of your love.

How we need to constantly seek God's fire. We need to hunger and thirst for the word of God. We need to pray earnestly and all the time. We need to live a life of holiness and complete obedience to God. Yes, how we need to have a great desire for the return of the Lord. How we need a true, real and steadfast faith in God. To burn for God, we need to love sacrificially. We cannot merely submit today and not tomorrow, for it will be like a flame that flickers a while, but is quenched or put out by the dust of life. Every day we need new fire. The world is seeking fire. The world is seeking love and authenticity. The world is seeking passion, answers, and hope. The world is seeking the power that frees and heals and delivers from the swamps of darkness. That is the fire God. So seek Him.

Of the Lord, we read in "Ezekiel 1: 27 Also from the appearance of His waist and upward I saw, as it were, the color of amber with the appearance of fire all around within it; and from the appearance of His waist and downward I saw, as it were, the appearance of fire with brightness all around. 28 Like the appearance of a rainbow in a cloud on a rainy day, so was the appearance of the brightness all around it. This was the appearance of the likeness of the glory of the Lord." This description shows that God consists of fire! His body is fire. That is why fire is so important. The fire is His presence.

So seek the fire. Yearn for His presence. And from sunrise to sunset, burn for God!

# Prophetic word: Embers of Revival

*As given on February 9, 2011*

As My people come up the Mountain (Isaiah 2), ablaze and set alight for My glory, and as they come up the Mountain carrying the torch of the Gospel, and as they come up My mountain to hear My voice, I will send down fire, and it shall consume My people who are called by My name. So says the Lord.

And I, the prophet of the Lord, see how the Breath of God – that beautiful Spirit who is known by the Hebrew tongue as Ruach – start to blow and I saw how embers like coals of fire start to blow away from the living flames [they who have come up to the mountain as living offerings] and I saw how it was as if these embers [coals of fire] were detaching themselves from the living flames. It reminded me of a blazing wood fire with the embers shooting forth, and as that ember touches you, how it burns. Those who have stood around a fire and have been touched by an ember shall know that there is a jolt of surprise when its heat is felt by naked skin.

God calls us to be such living flames, with the Ruach of God blowing within us, thus heating up the fire within so that the flame flickers higher. Can we imagine how powerful and how beautiful such embers will be when they are blown in the wind of the Spirit!

For I see how these embers go forth, and they are carried in the Spirit [on the wind], and they are carried across mountains, valleys, forests, and they are carried across the oceans. They are carried across borders, and they go into windows and through doors and into palaces and government buildings and churches and all places of worship. These embers of fire [they are so alive with God's Shekinah fire] are so alive and so powerful, and they go forth, unstoppable and unquenchable, and they come to rest on people. For I see people kneeling, people in the office, people speaking and people having a good time – people of all colour and race and tradition and culture – and when the embers fall upon them then that fire will be imparted, and there will be a jolt to their spirit and they shall have an encounter with the Living God.

For as we pray, as we serve Him, as we remain obedient, as we pursue Him, as we preach His Word, as we declare and proclaim, as we remain and abide in Him, then the Lord shall carry our prayers, and He shall carry the fire within us and He shall carry the prophetic utterances and proclamations and He shall carry our tears and He shall carry our cries and He shall carry our longing and yearning like embers of a fire on the wind. For as we come to Him as a beautiful aroma, and as we come to Him as a Living Sacrifice, and as we come to Him at the burning bush, how the Lord shall consume us and by that consumption, He shall light the fire, and the fire shall go forth from us, and His Spirit rises up in power.

And I see as these embers touch people, it shall be as gentle but as powerful as when the Dove rested upon Jesus at the time of the Baptism. Can we discern such divine reality People will be praying to other gods or they will be kneeling to false idols or they will be busy with the things of the world when the embers touch them and that fire of God shall RIP – YES CRIES THE LORD – RIP AND TEAR them away from the darkness and the veil that covers their sight shall be lifted so they may see and know the Living God!

Hallelujah! Let it be and let it be! Glory to God! But how we need to get up that mountain to be imparted with His Vision so that we may run with our mandate and so move in His Spirit and Truth to His

Glory! Set us ablaze! Set us alight! Let us burn Lord! Make us indeed Your servants of fire! And let the members of revival be carried by the Ruach Adonai.

# Sent the fire

October 31 is Reformation Day. This is the day when, in 1517, a German monk named Martin Luther (1483-1546) strode up to the church in Wittenberg and nailed his 95 'theses' (or propositions) to the church door. Luther chose to do this on October 31 as he knew the church would be full on the next day for All Saints' Day.

The Protestant Reformation was the 16th-century religious, political, intellectual and cultural upheaval that splintered Catholic Europe, setting in place the structures and beliefs that would define the continent in the modern era. It birthed the Protestant movement, and it called for a return to Sola scriptura ("by Scripture alone"), Sola fide ("by faith alone"), Sola gratia ("by grace alone"), Solus Christus or Solo Christo ("Christ alone" or "through Christ alone") and Soli Deo gloria ("glory to God alone").

October 31 serves as a reminder of how desperately we need in our days another and hopefully the last reformation, or at least a transformation, where we return to the ways of God, to His truth, His will and His Kingdom. A return to the upholding in the Spirit of God the five Solas, a return to the heart of God, a return to the Word, a return to the Great Commission and a return to the Upper Room so that we may again be filled and be led by the Spirit of God. Yes, a Bride on fire for God, and a Bride yearning only for His glorious presence!

Hundreds of years ago, Luther and so many other Reformers bravely challenged a system that had defined the beliefs of people for more than 1000 years. How we need brave warriors of the Word again that will again defy our times of apostasy, spiritual lawlessness, corruption and deception. For while this world weeps in agony and brokenness, the church sleeps in comfort and spiritual passivity. How we need again fierce and passionate disciples who will yield to no other king except Jesus, who will bow to no other truth than the Bible and who will not love their lives unto death for the glory of God. How we need servants of compassion, of love, of hope and kindness to wrest the tides of darkness so that the world may again see the light of Christ!

We can only truly survive the demonic storms and remain standing for God's truth when we are tested in God's fire! For there is boldness in His fire. There is courage in His fire. There is conviction in His fire. It is the fire that allows us to walk in reality if "Joshua 1:. 9 Have I not commanded you? Be strong and of good courage; do not be afraid, nor be dismayed, for the Lord your God is with you wherever you go."

The following hymn, Sent the Fire by William Booth, is my prayer in such a time where God is calling for His sons and daughters to arise for truth, to stand up for the liberty of Christ and to again share the whole counsel of God as intended and taught by Jesus our Lord and only true Saviour of a world hell bent of destruction.

*Thou Christ of burning, cleansing flame,*
*Send the fire, send the fire, send the fire!*
*Thy blood-bought gift today we claim,*
*Send the fire, send the fire, send the fire!*
*Look down and see this waiting host,*
*Give us the promised Holy Ghost;*
*We want another Pentecost,*
*Send the fire, send the fire, send the fire!*
*God of Elijah, hear our cry:*
*Send the fire, send the fire, send the fire!*
*To make us fit to live or die,*
*Send the fire, send the fire, send the fire!*
*To burn up every trace of sin,*

*To bring the light and glory in,*
*The revolution now begin,*
*Send the fire, send the fire, send the fire!*
*'Tis fire we want, for fire we plead,*
*Send the fire, send the fire, send the fire!*
*The fire will meet our every need,*
*Send the fire, send the fire, send the fire!*
*For strength to ever do the right,*
*For grace to conquer in the fight,*
*For pow'r to walk the world in white,*
*Send the fire, send the fire, send the fire!*
*To make our weak hearts strong and brave,*
*Send the fire, send the fire, send the fire!*
*To live a dying world to save,*
*Send the fire, send the fire, send the fire!*
*Oh, see us on Thy altar lay*
*Our lives, our all, this very day;*
*To crown the off'ring now we pray,*
*Send the fire, send the fire, send the fire!*

# Spontaneous word:
# Glorious Fire

As given in September 2009

Should it not be asked? Should it not be pondered? Who is this Mighty Lord who rules and reigns over universes, man, earth, skies, mountains, spiritual dimensions, angels and all things eternal and temporary? Should it not be asked and should it not be pondered as who this great God is who stretches forth His hand in great power to form, to give life, to change, to transform, to bind, to loosen, to heal, to deliver and to create? Should it not be considered, should it not be pondered who is this great God whom you serve, this God whom mankind has taken so lightly and this great God who have so often been pushed aside in the pursuit of man's desires, happiness and ambitions? Where is the reverence, the fear and the adoration of such holiness, purity and greatness?

Should it not be asked and should it not be considered how great our God is? The Holy Spirit asks of man in these very days, and it is He, oh Spirit here on earth, who asks of us to consider deeply who this God truly is whom we serve and to whom we bow the knee. How do we not make Him weep with our arrogance and pride, and cause Him pain and agony over our actions, our words and our nature? Shall we forget that once there was one who wanted to rise above the Mighty Lord, yet fell and was banished from the presence of His Mighty Glory and Glorious Fire? Why do we then seek such a path of seeking to raise ourselves on a pedestal, thus quenching the fire of the Almighty? Why then do we also seek to raise ourselves above this mighty One in our word and deed? Shall we not consider who this God is to whom we pray and bow our knees, yet so often abandon in our pursuits?

Shall we not consider and ponder the Glorious One who has pursued us? Shall we not consider and ponder, He is the Mighty One who has given us life and breath and hope and existence? Shall we not consider that we are made by His loving Hand and that all things bow before Him for now and ever and ever in the past? Shall we not consider who this Lord is, who has walked in the body of a man upon earth? Shall we not again consider the mighty wonders and the mighty works of the Great Lord I AM who walked with Israel, who walked with Abraham, Isaac and Jacob? Shall we not consider and ponder, asks the Spirit, the glorious nature of the ever-present and ever glorious Mighty One who is enthroned above all for all time and beyond all time?

Have we become so blind, and have we become so hard of hearing? Answer and state your case and your claim before the Mighty One, before the Glorious Son and before the Holy Spirit, why we rebel and seek other gods. Shall we make our claim and state our case as to why we have so many times forsaken the Great I AM, why we have turned away in our pursuits and have become so distant from Him? How have we not quenched His fire, rejected His love and run from His loving embrace!

Come, people, and remember whom you serve. Remember, consider, ponder and take a moment. Take a moment and remember who He is. He is God. He is real, alive and an all-consuming fire. For there is no other god, there is no other glory, there is no other hope, there is no other truth, there is no other life, there is no other healing, there is no other purpose but the life and truth and glory we find in God enthroned. So turn to Him, find Him again, and consider when you bow to whom you bow and to whom you pray.

For look, open your eyes, open your ears, and see Him, hear Him, hear the truth and see Him. As we open ourselves to His Presence and Glory, embraced by divine fire and life, we become saturated and immersed in His glorious nature. Such sweet and glorious fire and life! He is God, worthy of all our praise, adoration and worship. Seek Him day and night. For Jesus came to earth so that we may never take our eyes off the Holy One, so that our ears may be opened to hear His voice, to be His delight and to delight in Him!

Yes, we are called to be reborn by the Spirit, refined by fire, and to draw closer to His Glory. We are called to taste and see and live the essence of the Mighty One. In His Spirit, we come alive, and eternity stretches forth in the chambers of heart and spirit. In His fire, we are cleansed and purified to meet Him on the mountain. In His life, we rejoice. Abide in Him, for in intimate embrace restoration and resurrection power flows like liquid fire. Yes, He is Spirit, He is Love, and He is beautiful! Let Him be our delight and our desire!

So man, consider and ponder the Great I AM whom you serve, for He seeks your attention, for He seeks your love, and He seeks to dwell with us in His Spirit. For He is Glorious. Lord, may Your fire embrace in us – a sweet, intimate fire that draws us closer and deeper unto divine presence.

# The sweet joy of the fire

God continuously places in my spirit the absolute importance of the anointing of the Spirit. The anointing is the presence of the Spirit of God. And where the Spirit dwells and resides and manifests, we find the Shekinah fire! On Pentecost, the first disciples were touched by the Holy Spirit – infused with holy fire, heavenly passion and Kingdom power. The question is, how conscious and aware are we still of the anointing, thus the indwelling fire of the Spirit of God? Do we still consider it? Do we still take note of its absolute importance and its absolute necessity? How aware are we of God's presence in our lives?

The origin of anointing, by all accounts, stemmed from a practice of shepherds. Lice and other insects would often get into the wool of sheep, and when they got near the sheep's head, they could burrow into the sheep's ears and kill the sheep. So, ancient shepherds poured oil on the sheep's head to protect them from parasites and from harming themselves when infected. The anointing made the wool slippery, making it impossible for insects to get near the sheep's ears because the insects would slide off. From this, anointing became symbolic of blessing, protection, and empowerment.

The New Testament Greek words for "anoint" are chrio, which means "to smear or rub with oil" and, by implication, "to consecrate for office or religious service"; and aleipho, which means "to anoint." In Bible times, people were anointed with oil to signify God's blessing or call on that person's life (Exodus 29:7; Exodus 40:9; 2 Kings 9:6; Ecclesiastes 9:8; James 5:14). A person was anointed for a special

127

purpose—to be a king, to be a prophet, to be a builder and so on. In 2 Kings 9:6, we read: "So Jehu left the others and went into the house. Then the young prophet poured the oil over Jehu's head and said, 'This is what the Lord, the God of Israel, says: I anoint you king over the Lord's people, Israel.'"

Today, we are all anointed into the priesthood of God (1 Peter 2). We have been set apart, marked by the Holy Spirit (Ephesians 1:13). The reality is that the church will have no impact without the anointing. When we truly follow the Lord, serve Him, and when we yield as worshippers in Spirit and truth, we walk in the anointing. If we truly serve Him, we are set apart and consecrated for the work of the Lord. The anointing is not some magical powers endowed to us; it is simply a state of existence that comes from life completely and utterly yielding and submitting to the will and presence of God. Spiritual anointing with the Holy Spirit is conferred also upon Christians by God. It says in 2 Corinthians 1:21-22 - "And it is God who establishes us with you in Christ, and has anointed us, and who has also put his seal on us and given us his spirit in our hearts as a guarantee."

The anointing expresses the sanctifying influences of the Holy Spirit upon Christians who are priests and kings unto God (Revelation 1:6). Anointing is simply when we are under the influence, the power, the guidance and the divinity of the Holy Spirit. It is when we are saturated by holy fire, thus on fire to be empowered to do the work of God! We must walk so with the Lord that the anointing is smeared upon us, meaning we are saturated by the presence of God. You cannot buy the anointing. We cannot manipulate it or imitate it. The anointing comes from having a deep and real relationship with God.

To be anointed is to be set apart, empowered, or protected. It is being alive with holy fire from above. It is to carry the fire of God to set the world on fire with God's love and beauty. It means to dwell in the precious fire of the Lord. Let us also remember, many can be anointed, but there is a single Anointed One who made it possible for all – Jesus.

By the Covenant, we are now co-heirs of the everlasting Kingdom. Indeed by the indwelling of the Holy Spirit, anointing intends to set apart a person for divine use. In ancient times even places or things were anointed to be set apart. And so under the New Covenant, the Spirit of the Lord comes upon us to empower us to accomplish God's work.

If we are thus truly anointed, then we should be acting like we are set apart. We are supposed to be set apart from this world. We must be on fire for the Kingdom. Set apart from corruption and apostasy. In behaviour. In holiness and purity. If we are truly walking in the anointing, we walk in the fear of the Lord, not in the fear of this world. If we are truly walking in the anointing, our gaze is upon Jesus, upon His eternal Kingdom, upon the Truth of the Kingdom, upon all things noble, true, pure, right and fair.

If we are truly walking in the anointing, we walk in power and boldness. Not the power to be self-exalted or to be praised or lauded, but the power to shake the gates of hell, to set the captives free and to reach the lost. Yes, the power and boldness to drag the lost out of the flames of hell and to see the broken healed and the downtrodden restored. For to be anointed speaks of knowing you have no power, but power comes by the anointing activated by the infilling of the Holy Spirit. It says in the "Book of Jude verse 22 And have mercy on some, who are doubting; 23 save others, snatching them out of the fire." The anointing empowers and grants us such wisdom – to show mercy - but to also lead the lost out of the fire by proclaiming the Good News. We are indeed called to drive back the darkness in the fire of God to save others from the damnation fires of hell!

The anointing is the grace to walk in God's Truth, in His Ways, in His Presence, and it grants us the strength to seek His will and Kingdom above all. As mentioned, the anointing is not something that is apart from God, or some mythical potion or magic trick. It is the manifested reality of a living God within man, and where man has yielded to such a holy communion of abiding and surrendering.

We read in "Isaiah 10:27: And it shall come to pass in that day, that his burden shall be taken away from off thy shoulder, and his yoke from off thy neck, and the yoke shall be destroyed because of the anointing". God was giving this message to the Israelites concerning their enemies, the Assyrians. Through God's anointing, the Assyrian yoke was to be broken. That same promise the Lord gave the Israelites so many years ago to break bondage is in effect for you today if you will accept it. We of course also read in Matthew 11:28-30: "Come to me, all you who are weary and burdened, and I will give you rest. Take my yoke upon you and learn from me, for I am gentle and humble in heart, and you will find rest for your souls. For my yoke is easy and my burden is light."

When we abide in the Lord, we abide in the anointing. We abide in his holy and sweet fire that runs like a liquid in our veins. When we abide in the anointing, we find our rest in God, and all the strongholds and the bondages of the devil are broken. Under the anointing, we break free from the forces of darkness and slavery. Yes, in the anointing we have been set free, for indeed, those whom the son has set free is free indeed (John 8:36). For only the Truth of God sets us free (John 8:32), and Jesus is the Truth for He is the Word that became flesh. Glory to God!

If you will carry the yoke of Jesus, He promised you would learn of Him and find rest unto your soul. The Lord's yoke is one of love, understanding, security and protection—an easy yoke, one that makes the burdens light. The devil yokes us by fooling us to believe lies, to seek the world, to chase after fool's gold and to seek liberty and freedom in the carnal and the temporary instead of God. It is for freedom that Christ has set us free. It is written in "Galatians 1: 1 Stand firm, then, and do not let yourselves be burdened again by a yoke of slavery." Yes, by the Blood of Jesus we are set free, and by the anointing, we stay free, unburdened and untangled by the schemes and tricks of devilish horrors.

Throughout the ages, God has proven Himself as a yoke breaker. He looked at His people in Egyptian bondage, knowing their yoke was not of Him. In the slime pits the Israelites worked, making bricks for Pharaoh until their fingers were worn to nubs (according to Josephus). Adequate care was denied them; they had no freedom. The yoke they bore was severe, but God had promised Abraham hundreds of years earlier He would break that yoke and bring His people out of bondage into freedom.

It happened that a man tried to bring deliverance to his people before the appointed time. Moses rose to slay an Egyptian he had discovered beating a Hebrew; he sought to break the yoke without the anointing of God and it didn't work. Later, through that anointing, Moses broke the whole yoke. In the anointing of God, thus in the fire of God, we move in the power of God, in the liberty and the truth of God. To become rich or famous or exalted? No, but to fulfil the Great Commission and to be carriers of hope, of truth, of deliverance and restoration. None of this we are capable of in our strength or intellectual capacity, but only when God abides in us, for then we carry this message to a world spiritually dying and in great need of God.

It is declared in "Isaiah 61: The Spirit of the Lord God is upon me, because the Lord has anointed and commissioned me to bring good news to the humble and afflicted; He has sent me to bind up [the wounds of] the brokenhearted, To proclaim release [from confinement and condemnation] to the [physical and spiritual] captives and freedom to prisoners." This prophecy and truth were fulfilled by Jesus and it came into fulfilment in the lives of the disciples on the day of Pentecost. Isaiah 61 can also read "the anointing of the Lord is upon me", since the anointing comes with the infilling, thus the manifested work of the Holy Spirit. And by such a presence the fire is upon us! And such manifested work is the reality of Isaiah 11, for the Spirit of the Lord is the Spirit of understanding, wisdom, knowledge, might, counsel, and the fear of the Lord. The anointing is thus the manifested work of the fullness of the Spirit, therefore, the work of the knowledge, might, counsel, and power.

How we need a generation of believers seeking God and seeking the true inner power of the Holy Spirit to preach and teach the Truth, to be true disciples and walk in the glory and to the glory of God! Disciples walking in the fire for God! We need the Holy Spirit to empower and infuse us with holy fire and passion again to fulfil the Great Commission. How we need believers who are so on fire for the truth and who are on fire to walk in the ways of God! It is written in John 16 that the Holy Spirit has come to lead us in all truth. The reality is we need the anointing, thus the Holy Spirit operating in us because the Holy Spirit teaches by the anointing. We do not know the will of God by studying and weighing the pros and cons of a particular matter. We know the will of God by the anointing. The Holy Spirit communicates the mind of Christ to us. Indeed, we have the mind of Christ (1 Corinthians 2:16). As we yield to the anointing, then life flows freely from God. In the anointing, we learn, we know and we walk in the Truth. Remember, the anointing flows from God to the Body of believers, but only when they are directly under the Headship of God, thus abiding in Him and abiding by the Covenant.

Years ago, I read a book called Good Morning Holy Spirit by Ps Benny Hinn. It spoke deeply and passionately about the work of the Holy Spirit and of the anointing. It evoked in me a hunger to understand the anointing, to move with the Spirit and to seek Him above all else. At one time in the early 2000s, there was a lot of activity among Charismatics and Pentecostals when it came to the Holy Spirit. There was a great hunger, as seen in the Toronto and Brownsville revivals. Sure, some of the soaking meetings were a bit flaky and over the top, sprinkled with false intentions, but still, there was a real hunger for the Holy Spirit in people's lives. There was a true cry, a true need and a sincerity among many to be led by the Spirit, thus the anointing. Where are those days? We hardly hear any more sermons on the anointing, and when we do, it is misconstrued and distorted.

These days, there is a lot of talk about different levels of anointing, yet the Holy Spirit is the same in fullness upon all believers. God is an all-consuming fire. By His presence, we are called to be fully saturated by His fire. We talk about one person having a greater anointing than another, which is not true. God does not show favour, and neither is any mandate or calling greater than another. Truth is, the anointing of the Spirit never depletes or runs low or depreciates, unlike many other commodities such as oil, land or gold. But there is something we need to understand about the Anointing – as a believer who dwells in Jesus and who lives by His commandments and teachings and who follows the Spirit, it is not a question of how great the anointing is, but rather the flow of the Anointing. The more we yield and submit, the greater the flow!

How we need a generation of believers where the flow of the Anointing is the overflow so that the River of God within us becomes unstoppable and unquenchable! It is time for the believers to truly seek Him and to follow Him in greater spiritual depth and volume so that the Anointing of the Lord may overflow and by that overflowing touch the brokenness of the world and by that touch the power of God will restore, will mend, will deliver, will heal and will quench the thirst of the lost and the needy! Let it then overflow, and let the Lord pour into us like a never-ceasing rain and may the rivers of the Lord within us break its banks to touch the barrenness of a spiritually crippled world. Let it overflow! And in the overflowing, let us be set on fire for God. Amen

# Quenching the Spirit's fire

1 Thessalonians 5:19 - "Do not put out the Spirit's fire" (NIV)

The fire of God is the all-consuming power from the Almighty King to deliver, to save and to heal. It is the all-consuming power to renew, revive, and restore. It is the fire that purifies, sanctifies and refines.

The fire of God that is found throughout Scriptures is the very essence of God's awesome presence, and it is His awe-inspiring power. Within the fire lies the power that can bring down the strongholds of the enemy.

In the beginning, there was only darkness. There was nothingness; there was no life, no fish, no animals, no sky, no earth, no man, and no water. There was no light, and there was no oxygen.

In this blackness, the Spirit of God moved (Genesis 1:1). When creation was formed, the Spirit was present. Then God spoke, giving the command for light (a separation in the darkness). What happened when God the Father spoke? The fire fell. That is what happened. The Spirit is the fire of God; He is the one who executes the commands of God the Father. So when God spoke out of that nothingness, the Spirit moved, therefore fire moved and behold, creation unfolded.

There was light and there was darkness. There was day and night. The Spirit kept moving. The fire kept falling. God kept working. Land and water were made, then life, man, and animals.

Out of sheer nothingness, out of nothing but darkness, the earth came into existence. We live in a world that has astounded scientists, biologists and psychologists for centuries.

The Spirit executes this power and this creativity. The fire of God burns in the Spirit and burns in Christ. When the Spirit of the Living God therefore moves, so does that awesome fire move and act.

It is incredible to reflect that when Jesus Christ defeated death by rising from the grave, the Spirit of God was sent to earth to dwell among the people until the coming of Jesus. The same Spirit who moved at the beginning to create the earth makes His dwelling among us.

Through the anointing and indwelling of the Spirit, all the power of God Almighty, that same power manifested throughout time, can be released in the Spirit through us!

We are empowered to stand strong against the devil and sickness, death and sin.

Do not put out the Spirit's fire.

Believers, for too long, the fire has been watered down and has been extinguished by shutting the door to the Holy Spirit. For too long, the Spirit of God has not been allowed to move freely within our lives. For too long, the Spirit of God has been pushed to one side as believers try to do God's work in their own effort, believing they have the answers and the means to achieve their purpose.

We are grieving the Spirit every time we shut the door when we refuse the work of the Spirit. It is written that Jesus is the same yesterday, today and forever. Therefore, the Spirit, who is the embodiment of Christ, is also the same yesterday, today and forever. He is the same awesome Spirit that came upon Jesus, Samson, Moses, David, Daniel and all the prophets.

How on earth can we possibly quench the fire that burns in the Spirit?

The very fruits of the Spirit, the very gifts of the Spirit, are not dead and they have not passed away! How can they be if the Spirit is the same for all ages?

People seek truth, they seek knowledge, they seek understanding, they seek purpose, they seek wealth, they seek fulfilment, but they struggle, for they seek it in the world.

In the Spirit of God dwells all truth, all wisdom, all meaning, all creativity, all wealth, all power and all glory.

In the Spirit of God burns that consuming fire that is above all rule, authority, power or dominion on earth or in the spiritual realm.

We don't have to run around trying to find answers. We only have to invite Him in, submit to Him and let the fire of God freely burn in us. Then the ability to resist the devil shall flow like mighty streams from the throne room of God the Father!

The Holy Spirit wants to do so much through us so that we stay true to our calling. In His power and strength, we run the race and fulfil the Great Commission. But we need to be a people on fire for God! The ability of the Holy Spirit is endless, unlimited and beyond our human comprehension. We need to submit and let the fire flow.

We must not put out the fire of God!

# Pulpits aflame with righteousness

Alexis de Tocqueville, a French diplomat, political scientist and historian, wrote the following in his volume of work titled Democracy in America:

"I sought for the greatness and genius of America in her commodious harbors and her ample rivers – and it was not there . . . in her fertile fields and boundless forests and it was not there . . . in her rich mines and her vast world commerce – and it was not there . . . in her democratic Congress and her matchless Constitution – and it was not there. Not until I went into the churches of America and heard her pulpits aflame with righteousness did I understand the secret of her genius and power. America is great because she is good, and if America ever ceases to be good, she will cease to be great."

De Tocqueville, therefore, said that America was great because America was good, and America was good because the true Word of God was being preached from her pulpits. This was said in 1835. How times have changed. Do we truly find pulpits anymore aflame with righteousness, not just in America, but across the world? Do we still find those who have a true love for God's Word, even rebuking and correcting all kinds of evil, immorality, deception and wickedness in the land? Do we truly still find preachers and teachers of the Word on fire for the truth? Of course, there are such pulpits, but those pulpits are few and far between. So many are being swallowed by the tide of self-love, and the love for greed, power and money.

For a country to be great, and for a country to thrive, the true Word of God should be preached and should be the guiding light for the government, for business and for all modes of activity in society. God is life, and a nation that truly is led by the hand of God, following the moral compass of the Kingdom, shall be a nation that strives for righteousness, holiness and purity. How indeed we need a church presence that burns with God's righteousness and truth and holiness!

Look at the state of the world. We live in times of anarchy, apostasy, decadence, violence, chaos, immorality, debauchery and wickedness. We live in times of darkness, sickness, poverty and genocide. This is evident on every continent and in every nation. Is it not because the Church, in general, is no longer on fire for God? Is it not that are so few pulpits truly aflame with righteousness, declaring the uncompressing truth of God? Yet, these days, the pulpit is more concerned about political correctness, and with self-exaltation, self-hype and self-glorification. Across the world, all things immoral in the eyes of God have become moral and all things unnatural have become natural in the eyes of man. Where are the servants of God to correct such wickedness? Instead, churches are steadily condoning sin and iniquity, approving of evil, as we are more concerned about man's opinion than the Word of God. Pulpits have become quiet and silent on such matters, fearing man more than fearing God, as we are no longer interested in saving people from the flames of hell. Instead, we are more interested in a feel-good encounter Gospel, yet true discipleship continues to die in churches.

And so the world is hurled into darkness, aflame with moral corruption and spiritual bankruptcy, all because the true light of our Lord Jesus is hardly been shone from the pulpits. Where is the true cry for repentance, and how can we repent if the people no longer know what is right and wrong? Where is the chastisement to correct the ways of the people, and where is the holy fear of God in the nations any more?

2 Timothy 4 have become so true in our days when Paul wrote: "1 I charge you therefore before God and the Lord Jesus Christ, who will judge the living and the dead at His appearing and His kingdom: 2 Preach the word! Be ready in season and out of season. Convince, rebuke, exhort, with all longsuffering and teaching. 3 For the time will come when they will not endure sound doctrine, but according to their own desires, because they have itching ears, they will heap up for themselves teachers; 4 and they will turn their ears away from the truth, and be turned aside to fables. 5 But you be watchful in all things, endure afflictions, do the work of an evangelist, fulfill your ministry."

Sadly, sound Gospel is hardly been preached as so much false theology and teachings have evaded the pulpit. And so the people turn their ears away from the Truth that saves and sets free, only seeking a word that soothes and exalts the ego and the pride. Where are the men and women of God, on fire for God that convinces, rebukes and exhorts with all longsuffering and teaching?

For De Tocqueville, it was simple – a nation is great because of the power of God, but then God must be the God of the nation. And this only happens when a nation is truly led by the Word of God – undiluted and spoken as the Spirit of the Living God leads. Take a closer look at this world. It is burning with suffering and hate. Where is the light? Where is the truth anymore? For the pulpit has become about man and his selfish needs, and it is no longer about God. How we need to pray for the pulpits to become on fire again for our Lord and Saviour Jesus, and how the Truth needs to be preached again that sets us free. May the pulpits be on fire for God, no matter the cost.

This was what drove the Reformation – standing upon Scripture alone. And the Reformers were willing to suffer for the Truth. They were willing to challenge governments, even if they were branded heretics. Such men and women are becoming fewer in our times. We are bowing to man, to governments and to the devil's agenda as we are willing to accept the 30 silver pieces to betray the Lord.

In Ephesians 6, Paul declares: "13 Therefore take up the whole armor of God, that you may be able to withstand in the evil day, and having done all, to stand." Such evil times are upon us. It is a time of great darkness and the time of the falling away. We can only stand when we remain in the Truth of God, and in the Spirit of the Lord. All around us, the storms of wickedness rage, and so many people are being swept away in the tides of peril and terror, all because the pulpits are no longer aflame with righteousness.

God, may we burn with Your Spirit again, declaring the Truth of God as Your Spirit leads. May we remain standing on our ground, and not give up ground, and may we refuse to back down from the Truth. May we refuse to recant, no matter what people say or think of us. Grant us the strength to remain true to Your Truth in times of great evil, and may our words be salted and be aflame with Your divine touch. Amen

# No lack in the fire

The wonderful news is that where the revival waters of God flow, then there is no room for the devil, for dryness, for fear, or doubt! For where the fire of God burns, there is no lack! It says in "2 Timothy 1:7 that we have not been given a spirit of fear, but of love, a sound mind and of power." For the Spirit of God activates revival life and hope, and where the Spirit flows, there is indeed a yearning, a hunger and a longing for God's power, His mercy, His love and grace!

Yes, there is victory in the presence of God! Revival is the sweet touch of the Shepherd who leads us to green pastures and quiet rivers (which speaks of life). For where revival flows, there is liberty and life. There is freedom. For in God is our freedom from bondage, from slavery, from darkness and spiritual corruption. There is freedom and liberty in the sweet and powerful revival fire of God!

Isaiah 44 says, "3 For I will pour water on the thirsty land, and streams on the dry ground. I will pour out my Spirit on your offspring, and my blessing on your descendants." Oh yes, where God moves, there is no dryness! No lack. No need. No want. This is the reality of Matthew 6. It is the reality of Deuteronomy 2:7 that says, "The Lord your God has blessed you in all the work of your hands. He has watched over your journey through this vast wilderness. These forty years the Lord your God has been with you, and you have not lacked anything." Oh yes, God's Presence was with Israel even in the wilderness, and they lacked nothing. Of this we read in "Nehemiah 9:21: For forty years you sustained them in the wilderness; they lacked nothing, their clothes did not wear out nor did their feet become swollen."

Psalms also speak of no lack when we dwell with God. And make no mistake, revival is all about God's presence and abiding in such presence. We read for example:

Psalm 23:1 The Lord is my shepherd, I lack nothing.

Psalm 34:9: Fear the Lord, you his holy people, for those who fear him lack nothing.

Psalm 34:10: The lions may grow weak and hungry, but those who seek the Lord lack no good thing.

Psalm 91 makes it clear we are victorious in His Presence. The fire is His Presence. John 15 makes it clear that we grow spiritually to produce godly fruit when we abide in God. Revival is all about God. Dryness speaks of lack. It speaks of no life. It speaks of death. Yet Jesus Himself said He is the resurrection and the life. In John 10:10, He warned us about the thief but also said that God comes to give us life in abundance. Revival is God's Presence, and in such presence is hope, growth, victory and peace.

Isaiah 35 speaks of the blessed Way of Holiness. This is the Way of Jesus for He is the Way. This is the way of the narrow road of the Kingdom. And so we read:"1 The desert and the parched land will be glad; the wilderness will rejoice and blossom. Like the crocus, 2 it will burst into bloom; it will rejoice greatly and shout for joy. The glory of Lebanon will be given to it, the splendor of Carmel and Sharon; they will see the glory of the Lord, the splendor of our God … 5 Then will the eyes of the blind be opened and the ears of the deaf unstopped. 6 Then will the lame leap like a deer, and the mute tongue shout for joy. Water will gush forth in the wilderness and streams in the desert. 7 The burning sand will become a pool, the thirsty ground bubbling springs. In the haunts where jackals once lay, grass and reeds and papyrus will grow. 8 And a highway will be there; it will be called the Way of Holiness; it will be for those who walk on that Way. The unclean will not journey on it; wicked fools will not go about on it. 9 No lion will be there, nor any ravenous beast; they will not be found there. But only the redeemed will walk there, 10 and those the Lord has rescued will return. They will enter Zion with singing; everlasting joy will crown their heads. Gladness and joy will overtake them, and sorrow and sighing will flee away."

Revival is God's Presence manifested. It is God's Presence indwelling (Shekinah Glory) and changing hearts and minds. In His Presence is healing. In His Glory is deliverance. Where revival burns, there is joy, love, gladness and hope! Yes, there is no lack. There is no sickness. There are no bondages. No demonic strongholds can stand. Oh yes, to walk such a way speaks of God's splendour, of His holiness and might! There is victory in God's Presence, for revival is the manifestation of God's power and glory.

Of Jesus, we read in Isaiah 53:2: "He grew up before him like a tender shoot, and like a root out of dry ground. He had no beauty or majesty to attract us to him, nothing in his appearance that we should desire him." Oh yes, from humble beginnings (the dry ground), the Lord grew in stature and might and strength. In God, we are called to walk in His fullness. And by such a reality, we are not merely a tender root. We are not bound to what is dry and forgotten. We are victorious in the glory of His provision, in the mercy of His love and the grace of His acceptance.

Psalm 1 says, "1 Blessed is the one who does not walk in step with the wicked or stand in the way that sinners take or sit in the company of mockers, 2 but whose delight is in the law of the Lord, and who meditates on his law day and night. 3 That person is like a tree planted by streams of water, which yields its fruit in season and whose leaf does not wither— whatever they do prospers." Oh yes, in God's presence we are fed, nourished and strengthened by God. This is the reality of revival – for revival speaks of divine nourishment, of divine hope and divine conviction of Romans 8.

Isaiah 55 declares, "1 Come, all you who are thirsty, come to the waters; and you who have no money, come, buy and eat! Come, buy wine and milk without money and without cost." In God's presence, there is no more spiritual thirst. Revival is the fulfilment of spiritual need and want. Matthew 5:6 says, "Blessed are those who hunger and thirst for righteousness, for they will be filled." Revival is truly about yearning for God, His Kingdom, and His ways of righteousness. And in such yearning is our joy and contentment and peace. Revival is the fulfilment of "John 6:35: Then Jesus declared, "I am the bread of life. Whoever comes to me will never go hungry, and whoever believes in me will never be thirsty."

In Matthew 12 we read "When an impure spirit comes out of a person, it goes through arid places seeking rest and does not find it." Nothing demonic is to be found in the living waters of revival. It is not found in the sweet delight of God's presence. Where there is dryness, there is lack, and here you will find the devil operates. For he is the thief that steals, kills and destroys to produce lack, dryness and an arid spiritual state. But in God we experience not such dryness, or lack, or want, for in the Kingdom is our deliverance and our refuge from the darkness. In the fire of God, there is a sweet desire to know more of God. In His fire rests our strength and hope.

# A call to fan the flame

If we look at the times we are living in, then God is certainly waking up people spiritually. It is not just about bringing people back to God, but also strengthening people's spiritual walk with God, and really bringing people back to a point of intimacy and passion on a spiritual level. I believe some believers who have stayed close to the Lord have also let the inner fire run cold, so this is a time that serves as a call to the deeper and back to the heart of God.

The apostle Paul wrote in 2 Timothy 1:6: "I remind you to fan into flame the gift of God, which is in you." What is the gift of God in us? In the very next Scripture, it says: "7 For God did not give us a spirit of timidity or cowardice or fear, but [He has given us a spirit] of power and of love and of sound judgment and personal discipline [abilities that result in a calm, well-balanced mind and self-control]."

Let us be reminded that before we were born again, our spirit was completely dead, cold, and empty. But when we believed in Christ, He as the life-giving Spirit came to be mingled with and live in our spirit. Our regenerated human spirit was ignited with the divine fire of the Spirit of God. The precious gift of God in us is our spirit indwelt by the Holy Spirit. This is the gift we must fan into flame. Yes, our regenerated spirit was ignited by the divine fire of the Spirit. But after we're saved, our zeal for the Lord may eventually fade. We're not as hot and burning as when we first received the Lord. But Romans 12:11 exhorts us not to be "slothful in zeal, but be burning in spirit, serving the Lord." Dear believers, the Lord wants us to be hot, burning in our love for Him and our service to Him. This is why we need to fan our spirit into flame!

Yes, many in this world still rebel against God, while some believers have completely abandoned their faith, but then you also get those who still serve Him and trust Him, yet that inner fear of a life submitted to God has run cold. I am again reminded of Revelation 3:16, which says: "So, because you are lukewarm—neither hot nor cold—I am about to spit you out of my mouth". This scripture is about a spiritual life that is in limbo, neither alive with God nor dead. It has become stagnant, passive, and the fire is slowly fading.

How the Lord is again calling for believers in this time and age to fan the flame again! How the Lord is calling for people to seek Him like never before, reconnect with the Spirit, and let the fire of God burn, yes burn! For many, where there was once a burning flame, there is now only embers. Yet when you fan the embers, they then become alive again!

Leviticus 6:12 (New King James Version) says the following: "And the fire on the altar shall be kept burning on it; it shall not be put out. And the priest shall burn wood on it every morning, and lay the burnt offering in order on it; and he shall burn on it the fat of the peace offerings." In the Old Testament, the fire never had to die on the altar, because the aroma and sacrifice must be a constant reminder of the covenant between the people and God.

Just so, we are the living sacrifices who have laid down the old life. The flame must never die within us, so that we may be a constant sweet aroma unto God, and that there is a constant manifestation of the living Covenant sealed by the Holy Spirit (2 Corinthians 2:22). Constantly, we must yield, submit and walk in the Spirit. For it says in 2 Corinthians 2:14: But thanks be to God, who always leads us in triumph in Christ, and through us spreads and makes evident everywhere the sweet fragrance of the knowledge of Him.

Yes, our lives must always be connected to the Spirit of God. We must be infused into God so that He truly abides in us and we abide in us! There is a beautiful song by Brian Doerksen called Light the Fire Again. The lyrics are as follows: Don't let our love grow cold; Cause I'm calling out; Light the fire again; Don't let our vision die; I'm calling out; Light the fire again; You know my heart, my deeds; I'm calling out; Light the fire again; I need Your discipline; I'm calling out; Light the fire again.

Yes, Lord, light the fire again! May we again be a people who walk by the Spirit, who talk by the Spirit, who function, operate and minister in the Spirit! May we again become aware of the fusion of our spirit with the Holy Spirit, and may we truly burn for God again. Lord, You are an all-consuming fire. May it burn in us, Lord, and grant us the strength to truly fan the flame!

# Spontaneous word:
# Glorious eternal and
# divine God of light

Light cascades, swirling and illuminating from the throne room, transcendent, translucent, as with divine power and glory it flows over the marble floor, beautiful, deeply true, where no shade, no shadow, no fear, no pain, no death and no hurt hides or resides.

From the glorious throne upon which the Almighty is seated, the light and fire cascades, the light flows, the light blooms, strong and true, blinding to the human eye, overpowering, mesmerizing, yet deep within the light life eternal and life forever flows and breathes so holy – for this glorious light, not tangible, not of substance, not of earthly bound value, flows from the Almighty, yet the light is He, and the light is within Him, for He is the great illumination, for He is glory, for He is the ever-present and ever eternal one from which light and life flow.

He is the light and life, and as the light cascades and swirls and flows, at times like liquid fire, yet not fire, yet not warm to the touch, yet golden, yet orange, yet not the orange of our horizons, yet not golden as our earthly nectar, for it is translucent, transcendent, yet it swirls, cascades, for it is holy and pure, without flaw, for it is God, and in God, there is no darkness, there is no fear, there is no doubt, for in Him the eternity of eternal joy abounds and it flows like fiery light. A light that is of the Spirit and is Spirit – over those who yearn for thee, oh Lord, here on earth, soil made by Your Hand, and it flows and nurtures and feeds those who have overcome and who walk among the shade and the warmth of gardens of life and heaven of peace to know and breathe His majesty and love.

Such is the glorious way and the glorious touch and the glorious holy nature of the One on the throne from which the light and the life, one, pure, holy, forever, eternal, beyond word or thought flow. Such is the nature of the One who abounds heaven and universe, the One whose love – a love sweet in Him and He being the love – cascades and flows, swirling and illuminating, from His throne, from His hands, from His very essential being of Spirit of which light and life are intertwined, as it flows and cascades with such beauty and such worth and such holy purity over the souls and the yearning hearts of those who still on green pastures roam. These children, dear to His heart and close to His throne, are renewed by His fire, love and beauty, and they are encouraged, strengthened, lifted, and enfolded daily by the glorious One, in whom is love, in whom is the ever-flowing light, the cascading life.

For in Him, and His glorious Son and in the glorious Spirit there abides and rest but only the abounding and ever eternal peace and joy – yet joy and peace beyond the human comprehension or the human understanding. In the glorious One, enthroned, the Trinity, the fiery light, intangible, unfathomable, yet cascading and flowing, rises and rises to a glorious crescendo as if carried on the wings of the morning light, as it enfolds those who rise with Him with the morning.

It is true, for He, the glorious One, abides in His children toiling and striving on hard soil, yet the same light of magnificence, radiating and glowing from the Trinity - that same light so true and that same life and that same love so beautiful yet so illuminating and intangible - fills our hearts of blood and flesh. For as the glory and the cascading divine light and life in Him pours and washes, so the great One cascades divinely into us morning by morning, day by day, night by night, for it clings to our soul and our spirit, and it flows freely, and it flows deeply, into the crevices and caverns of our pain and hurt.

Yet, where the great One flows, the eternal God of mine heart so true, there is no darkness or shade or pain or shadow, for as the fiery light so holy so intangible washes and cleanses wounds so deep, once cleansing and washing wounds of our Lord Jesus, so this light and this glorious illumination of our God touches and nurtures where tears have dried, where pain resides and where longing is birthed.

Such is the love and such is the nature of the Great I AM, the eternal lover of our souls, in whom we delight, and who stretches that hand of eternal glory, just as Jesus stretches forth His marked hands, just as the Spirit stretches forth His hand, embracing, holding, loving, caressing and healing.

Such is He, who is the light and the love, for within Him we may take our rest and peace, for the shades and the haunting flee, for as the light and holiness flows and cascades in heaven and beyond, so His glorious nature and glorious love cascades into our souls, illuminating, lifting and easing the burden.

In Him, the darkness flees and the great glory abounds. And so He, the glorious One, stretches forth His hand. Shall we abide in Him and find our rest? Shall we seek His touch of love and embrace His fire of beauty and glory? Embrace and be known by Him in intimacy, for in intimacy the fire burns and life resides.

# Deliverance by fire

When it comes to deliverance in the church, you get all kinds of weird and strange ideas, concepts and practices. Most of them are simply laughable at their foolishness, others are downright ridiculous, and some are even scary because it is more like evil fighting evil!

Deliverance by fire has also become like a buzzword in the church. Often, you will find someone who is doing the apparent deliverance, screaming "fire, fire" at the person who needs to be set free. But what is strange is that so often there is no name of Jesus even used! Fire in itself as an element does not set anyone free, but only Jesus! For John 8:32 says the truth of God sets someone free. Not love, but the truth. Not fire, but only the truth, and Jesus is the truth. There is absolutely no point of screaming "fire, fire" if we are detaching the natural element of fire from God! We are then entering the territory of the pagans and the witches that attempt to control and manipulate the elements for their own twisted and distorted agendas!

The dubious practices of deliverance by fire have been gaining strength in continents like Africa. You will find people doing deliverance for themselves and on others by screaming stuff like "catch fire". This implies the demonic strongholds or the demon itself must catch fire. I have indeed, over the years, witnessed many such strange and weird practices when it comes to deliverance by fire. Yes, people think that if you scream "fire", the demons will react and people will be set free.

It is the power and presence of God that brings forth deliverance and healing, nothing else. Oh yes, we can certainly pray for the fire of God to bring forth a cleansing and deliverance and to break a stronghold, but then the fire is not detached from God. The fire is God's presence. It is the presence of the Holy Spirit. We cannot manipulate fire to bring forth any kind of deliverance. The power is in the name of Jesus, not in the name of fire!

So we must be very careful to listen to God and to remain grounded in the Word of God. We must not be swayed by all kinds of strange practices and teachings. Deliverance for the church has become a minefield of dubious ideas and practices, and so often it resembles more a circus than anything else. Yes, the fire of God is the presence of God, and we must yearn and seek His indwelling fire by the Spirit, yet we must not become so spiritual that we lose touch with the reality of God and His Word. Jesus never screamed "fire, fire" at the man possessed by Legion. The power is in God and in His Name. Let us remain true to the Word and true to God by being led by the Spirit of God.

# Contagious revival fire

There is a kind of fear that has ruled this age—fear of what spreads, fear of what is caught, fear of what passes unseen from hand to hand and breath to breath. The world has become cautious, guarded, sterilised by anxiety over contagion. But Heaven has never been afraid of what is contagious.

From the beginning, God designed His Kingdom to spread, not like a sickness that destroys, but like fire that transforms. Revival is not a theory, not a moment, not a controlled experience. Revival is a divine contagion. It is a holy infection. It is the unstoppable transmission of glory from vessel to vessel, life to life, heart to heart. The question is not whether something will spread in this generation. The question is what is spreading through us.

For God's children are not called to be spiritually sterile. They are not called to be sealed away from impact. They are called to be carriers, therefore, living hosts of divine fire, saturated with the presence of God until everything they touch begins to shift under the weight of glory. This is the nature of revival fire: it is contagious by design.

One spark from the altar ignites a prophet. One burning coal touches unclean lips and transforms a voice. One upper room experience turns fearful followers into flames that cannot be contained. And suddenly, ordinary men and women become walking atmospheres of heaven. When the world speaks of contagion, it speaks of loss of control. But when God speaks of contagion, He speaks of multiplication of glory.

We were never meant to merely believe in revival; we were meant to carry it. To breathe it. To walk into rooms and shift the spiritual temperature. To lay hands not as ritual, but as release. To speak not empty words, but ignited decrees. To live so saturated in the presence of God that even proximity becomes transformation. This is the mystery of holy fire: it spreads without permission. It ignores boundaries. It moves through vessels that yield themselves, and it consumes everything that is not aligned with life.

So let the question confront every believer: If fear has been contagious in the world, why has fire not been more contagious in the Church? Because revival fire is not waiting for permission, it is waiting for surrender. When a people become fully yielded, when altars are rebuilt within the heart, when prayer becomes breath and worship becomes lifestyle, then contagion returns to its original purpose: not to spread death, but to spread divine life. And such people become dangerous to darkness, not because of volume, but because of saturation.

You cannot quarantine fire. You can only host it or resist it. And those who host it become carriers of awakening, bearers of glory, and walking evidence that the Kingdom of God is still contagious. Let it spread.

# About the Author

Ps Riaan Engelbrecht is the founder of Avishua Ministries, the vice-president of Lighthouse Ministries International and the station manager of Lighthouse Radio. His ministry deals primarily with the prophetic, but he also has a passion to teach the Truth of the Lord Jesus and His Kingdom for only the Truth of the Lord sets us free (John 8:32). He is also a qualified and seasoned journalist.

Read more at https://avishuaministries.wixsite.com/avishua.